MILITARY MIGHT AND GLOBAL INTERVENTION

Meddling or Peacemaking?

Erin L. McCoy and Adam Woog

Cavendish Square
New York

Published in 2020 by Cavendish Square Publishing, LLC
243 5th Avenue, Suite 136, New York, NY 10016

Library of Congress Cataloging-in-Publication Data

Names: Woog, Adam, 1953- author. | McCoy, Erin L., author.
Title: Military might and global intervention : meddling or peacemaking? / Adam Woog and Erin L. McCoy.
Description: First edition. | New York : Cavendish Square, 2020. | Series: Today's debates | Includes bibliographical references and index.
Identifiers: LCCN 2018056901 (print) | LCCN 2018057261 (ebook) | ISBN 9781502644794 (ebook) | ISBN 9781502644787 (library bound) | ISBN 9781502644770 (pbk.)
Subjects: LCSH: Humanitarian intervention. | Peacekeeping forces.
Classification: LCC JZ6369 (ebook) | LCC JZ6369 .W66 2020 (print) | DDC 341.5/84--dc23
LC record available at https://lccn.loc.gov/2018056901

Editorial Director: David McNamara
Copy Editor: Michele Suchomel-Casey
Associate Art Director: Alan Sliwinski
Designer: Christina Shults
Production Coordinator: Karol Szymczuk
Photo Research: J8 Media

CONTENTS

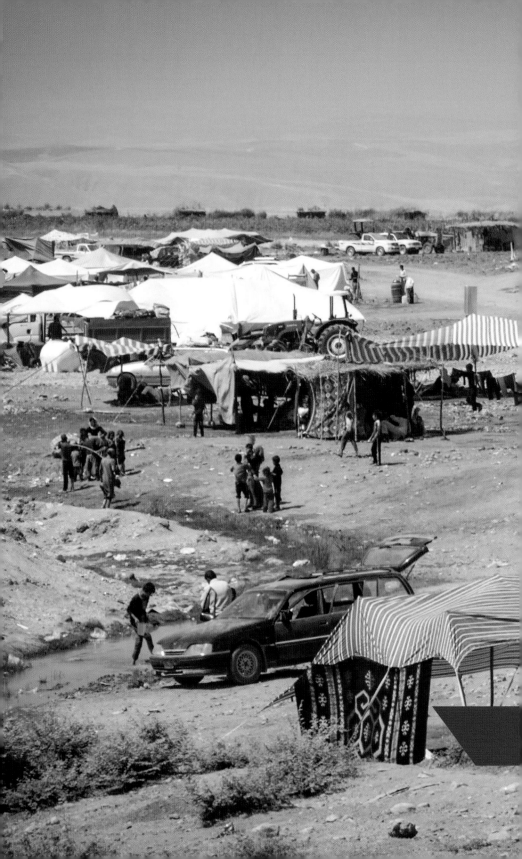

INTRODUCTION

It was a humanitarian crisis threatening thousands of lives, and if anyone was going to come to the rescue, they had to act quickly. In August 2014, forty thousand people had fled the area of Sinjar, Iraq, as fighters with terrorist organization the Islamic State of Iraq and Syria (ISIS) closed in around them. Now, they were trapped on a mountain, surrounded by ISIS fighters, without access to food and water. These people were members of the Yazidi minority group in Iraq. They had faced persecution for centuries because of their unique religious beliefs, and now, ISIS was perpetrating horrible crimes against them, including murder and sexual assault—all because they didn't share the same religious beliefs as ISIS

Opposite: Yazidi refugees enter Zakho, Iraq, in 2014. The Yazidi people came under attack from Islamic State fighters in 2014; the United States intervened to help them.

members. US president Barack Obama would, within days of the attack on Sinjar, declare these to be acts of genocide—that is, the systematic and intentional murder of a group of people based on racial, ethnic, cultural, or religious prejudice.

When acts of violence are taking place in one country, it is not always clear what other countries should do. Should they intervene militarily, sending in soldiers, weapons, and fighter planes? Should they intervene nonviolently, sending only food and supplies to those most in need? Is it better to simply let each nation work out its own problems? Each of these questions has a complex answer that depends on the particular situation—and also depends on whom you ask, since opinions can vary widely.

In the case of the attacks on the Yazidi, President Obama made a swift choice: on August 7, 2014, days after the violence against the Yazidi had begun, he authorized limited airstrikes to help save those Iraqi civilians trapped on the mountain. He explained why he felt the United States was obligated to step in:

> When we face a situation like we do on that mountain— with innocent people facing the prospect of violence on a horrific scale, when we have a mandate to help—in this case, a request from the Iraqi government—and when we have the unique capabilities to help avert a massacre, then I believe the United States of America cannot turn a blind eye. We can act, carefully and responsibly, to prevent a potential act of genocide.

Some might argue that these airstrikes were necessary to prevent brutal violence and that they were effective in helping many escape. Others might insist that there should have been more military intervention, considering that thousands of the 6,800 Yazidis who were kidnapped remained missing for years afterwards, during which time many were subjected to horrifying torture, sexual abuse, and enslavement. Still others might contend that the United States had no business intervening in a conflict on foreign soil. While it is impossible to be certain which of these opinions is correct, it is possible to understand each side of the issue.

Reasons for Intervention

The motivations for armed intervention typically fall into one of three categories: profit, self-defense, or the defense of other nations. Armed intervention, for these purposes or to other ends, has been part of history for as long as records have been kept. J. Bryan Hehir, a professor of religion at Harvard University, put it succinctly: "The use of force has been the core issue in the history of empires, nations, and states." In some cases, military incursions have been undertaken in defense against a dire threat or to alleviate suffering. In other cases, the reasons can be far less noble: to gain land, property, or resources, or to spread a particular ideology or religion.

Armed intervention, however, is not the only type of intervention that takes place. The international community will often step in during a violent conflict to offer food and medical aid to civilians and victims. Whether this type of aid is enough during a humanitarian crisis remains a matter of debate and can very much depend on the situation.

Whatever the cause, intervention across borders is still very much a part of today's world and still of vital concern to everyone. Even for citizens of a nation like the United States, which has not experienced war with another country within its borders in more than 150 years, involvement in armed conflict can be a major factor in their lives. There is, of course, the obvious tragedy of the loss of human life—perhaps including one's family members—on either side of the conflict. Beyond this, a conflict in a faraway nation can dramatically affect daily life, even for civilians, because of economic hardship or political upheaval.

Total figures are difficult to determine, and estimates vary widely, but researchers at the Institute for Health Metrics and Evaluation estimate that there were 5.4 million war-related deaths in thirteen war-affected countries between 1955 and 2002. (The survey's scope begins a decade after World War II, when somewhere between 50 million and 70 million people died.) Since 2002, more than 1.1 million people around the world have died because of conflict and terrorism.

Alternatives to Conflict

Armed intervention is often (but not always) carried out for reasons said to be humanitarian and by powerful nations operating in smaller developing countries. In today's world, it is generally accepted, by individual nations and by the globe's chief international regulatory organization, the United Nations, that such armed intervention is a drastic step for resolving disputes, one that is often just short of outright war. Before taking such a step, responsible leaders of nations will exhaust other forms of persuasion. The primary methods countries use before this final resort, as in Libya in 2011, include diplomacy, appeals to international legal bodies, and sanctions, such as restrictions on trade and travel.

A note is necessary here on terminology. The lines dividing the concepts of armed intervention, armed conflict, and war are blurry; they have shifted over the years, and many definitions have been suggested. Simply put, war could be considered an extreme case of armed conflict. Furthermore, some scholars make a distinction between military intervention and armed intervention; in this book, the terms are used interchangeably. Likewise, there can be subtle distinctions among governmental units—a nation, a country, and a state—but again the terms are used here interchangeably.

In any given situation, there are powerful arguments for and against the use of armed intervention. The negative aspects of armed intervention are clear, but there are times when many believe it is the only option. When President Obama accepted the Nobel Peace Prize in December 2009, he spoke plainly about the necessity, in some grave cases, for its legitimate use. He stated:

> *We must begin by acknowledging the hard truth: We will not eradicate violent conflict in our lifetimes. There will be times when nations—acting individually or in concert—will find the use of force not only necessary but morally justified …*
>
> *For make no mistake: Evil does exist in the world. A non-violent movement could not have halted Hitler's armies. Negotiations cannot convince al-Qaeda's leaders to lay down their arms. To say that force may sometimes be necessary is not a call to cynicism—it is a recognition of history; the imperfections of man and the limits of reason.*

There's no simple formula here. However, we must try as best we can to balance isolation and engagement, pressure and incentives. As Obama noted, the complex issues and tough questions that surround armed intervention are nothing new. The roots of these questions go far back in history.

It is therefore by studying past interventions that we can gain a deeper understanding of the many sides to this debate. A careful exploration of military and nonmilitary interventions throughout history will reveal the ways in which each succeeded and failed to achieve its aims.

Chapter One

MILITARY INTERVENTION THROUGHOUT HISTORY

Armed intervention has perhaps been part of the international political landscape since the invention of armies. The armies of Alexander the Great, Julius Caesar, and Genghis Khan all invaded other nations and territories—often to achieve greater power and gain new territory. However, since the modern concept of what a nation is emerged in the nineteenth century, ideas and policies about what role nations should play in the affairs of others have been undergoing a profound transformation.

It is only in modern times that laws, codes of conduct, and other agreements have come into play regarding military intervention. Typically, diplomats

Opposite: European leaders gather in 1815 for the Congress of Vienna as they work to bring an end to the Napoleonic Wars.

and leaders of the countries in question, along with representatives of disinterested nations, meet peacefully to set laws and reach mutually agreeable terms.

The Congress of Vienna

The object of these mutually agreeable terms is to maintain and keep in check the balance of power, in large part to prevent any one nation or coalition of nations from initiating unwarranted aggression. One of the most significant conferences in modern times to address this issue was the Congress of Vienna. This milestone in the history of European military and political negotiations offers a convenient starting point for a discussion of the relationship between politics and armed intervention, especially in the West.

The Congress of Vienna met in the wake of a series of cataclysmic changes in Europe in the late eighteenth and early nineteenth centuries: the French revolutionary wars, the Napoleonic Wars, and the collapse of the Holy Roman Empire. As a result of these political and military events, the continent's geographic borders were controversial and the balance of power—that is, a balance that would prevent any one country from dominating—was precarious and volatile.

In the wake of this uncertainty, the leaders of Europe's most powerful nations organized the first major conference of the era designed to address the balance of political and military power: the Congress of Vienna. During 1814 and 1815, their representatives gathered in Austria's capital to settle these issues.

The five major nations represented were the United Kingdom, the Austrian Empire, Prussia, France, and Russia. Other powers, including Spain, Portugal, and Sweden, were involved in discussions on specific issues, primarily concerning disputes with other nations over borders and colonial possessions. However, they were not full participants in the conference and did not take part unless their interests related directly to an issue.

The primary goals of the discussions were closely interrelated. The participants in the Congress hoped to foster peace across Europe and to find ways to prevent hostile interventions in the future. One of the major agreements reached, which concerned physical land borders, resulted in significant changes to the continent's geopolitical map. In large part, the redrawing was intended to curtail future border disputes. Among other changes, the conference created new boundaries for France, the Netherlands, and various regions of the Rhine Valley, Italy, and the German province of Saxony.

Despite such changes, however, the delegates could not agree on a firm solution to the question of balancing power. This issue was precarious then, and it remains precarious today. Chancellor Otto von Bismarck, the dominant figure in nineteenth-century Prussian/German politics and a major player in European diplomacy, recognized well the problems embedded in this issue. In 1880, noting the importance of being part of a controlling majority, he commented, "All politics reduces itself to this formula: try to be one of three, as long as the world is governed by the unstable equilibrium of five great powers."

New Global Powers

Several nations of Europe dominated world affairs during the nineteenth century, although the balance of power between them shifted back and forth. For a significant period, the United Kingdom was preeminent, in large part because it boasted superior naval power and was able to maintain extensive colonial holdings in Africa and Asia. In the 1870s, a new force emerged on the scene: an alliance formed by the unification of Prussia, the German Confederation, Bavaria, and smaller German states into a single entity, the German Empire. The new coalition had tremendous potential for aggression if it chose that path—a possibility sometimes referred to as the German problem.

Meanwhile, thanks in large part to their increasing industrialization, some states outside the traditional power bases in Europe were emerging as major global players. Preeminent among these were two nations that had been only minor figures in the nineteenth century: Japan and the United States.

The United States owed its ascent to its success in the Spanish-American War, fought in 1898. It was this war, ostensibly triggered by efforts to aid anti-Spanish rebel forces in Cuba, that led to the US annexation of the Philippines and other regions formerly held by Spain.

Similarly, Japan was expanding its influence in Asia: following its victory in the Russian-Japanese War, Japan essentially took control of Korea, Taiwan, and other parts of Asia. It was becoming clear that the potential for initiating armed intervention was present well beyond the five European powers and their colonies.

Japan and the United States had a chance to flex their new political and military muscles between 1898 and 1901, when Chinese rebels engaged in a conflict known as the Boxer Rebellion. This conflict had arisen in response to the West's desire to expand its colonial empires into China. The Chinese were also protesting the overall spread of outside religious and cultural influences. Japan, the United States, the five major powers, and Italy formed the Eight-Nation Alliance, which authorized a multilateral military force that quashed the uprising.

World War I and Rebalancing Power

Roughly a decade and a half after the end of the Boxer Rebellion came the long, bloody conflict of World War I, a devastating

British forces move through Bapaume, France, during a battle in the late summer of 1918.

event that resulted in some fifteen million deaths and forever changed the international balance of power. US president Woodrow Wilson called the European conflict "the war to end all wars," a term reflecting his hope that the world would never again see such destruction.

The causes of World War I are complex and many, but one primary factor was a massive arms race (particularly when it came to naval strength) between Germany and England. Other factors included ongoing aggression across national borders on the part of Germany and its supporters. These factors, in turn, were directly descended from the "German problem" that had developed late in the preceding century.

Armed intervention, especially when it escalates into full-blown war, has a clear and terrible aftermath. A large-scale rebalancing of political and military power is by no means the only consequence of war. There are catastrophic costs for everyday people on both sides—in the case of World War I, millions of deaths and the utter destruction of cities and huge areas of land. These costs, of course, have been exacted since ancient times, through such conflicts as the medieval Hundred Years' War, the Napoleonic Wars, and on into the present day.

World War I, often called the Great War, began in 1914. It pitted the Allies against the Central Powers. At the outbreak of conflict, the primary Allied nations were France, the Russian Empire, and England; the United States provided only monetary aid until 1917, when it actively joined the fighting. The primary entities comprising the Central Powers, meanwhile, were the German Empire, the Austro-Hungarian Empire, the Ottoman Empire, and the Kingdom of Bulgaria. When the conflict ended in 1918, the Allied nations emerged victorious.

In the wake of the war, extensive talks were held to draw up peace treaties, agree on financial settlements for war damages, and establish new political boundaries. The defeated Central Powers were excluded from these talks. Russia was also excluded since it had already negotiated a separate treaty with Germany. These discussions resulted in the dissolution of German power and the end of the Austro-Hungarian Empire, which was carved up into several small and relatively weak states including Czechoslovakia, Austria, Hungary, and Yugoslavia.

One of the most important documents to come out of these talks, signed after six months of negotiation, was the primary peace agreement, the Treaty of Versailles. Among other things, this treaty established the League of Nations, a permanent international agency representing a majority of the world's powers. Anticipating the formation of the United Nations, the League of Nations was designed to foster disarmament and negotiation as alternatives to future armed conflict. It declared itself authorized to "take any action that may be deemed wise and effectual to safeguard the peace of nations."

The league was organized so that five of the world's dominant nations were awarded permanent seats on the League of Nations Council, effectively acting as the organization's executive body. The United States was not a member of the council, however, and never joined the league in any capacity. Despite protracted negotiations, the Senate remained wary of meddling in the affairs of other nations and vice versa. One of the league's strongest opponents, Idaho senator William E. Borah, declared, "[By joining, the United States would have] forfeited and surrendered, once and for all, the great policy of 'no entangling alliances' upon which the strength of this Republic has been founded for 150 years."

The rejection by Congress of the opportunity to join the new organization was intensely disappointing to President Wilson, who had been one of the league's principal architects. The league thus began its work without American participation and with only four permanent members on its executive council: England, France, Italy, and Japan.

The organization had some notable successes in the ensuing years, including the resolution of a border conflict between Greek and Yugoslavian troops in Albania. The league also successfully negotiated the end to forced labor practices in Liberia, whose government had been sanctioning the export of ethnic minorities to French and British colonies as virtual slaves. This humanitarian triumph notwithstanding, the League of Nations was often severely hampered in its ability to effect real change because it had little ability to back up its resolutions with force. Most significantly, in historical terms, it was unable to stop the rise of Nazi Germany and thus failed to prevent another devastating war.

The Emergence of the United Nations

The war, of course, was World War II, which broke out in 1939. In this conflict, Nazi-controlled Germany joined forces with Japan and Italy to form the Axis powers. Pitted against them were the Allied forces: initially the United Kingdom and France, followed later by the successor to the Russian Empire, the Soviet Union, as well as the United States, China, and (to a lesser extent) many other countries.

When the war ended in 1945, the victors were the Allies, with the United States, the United Kingdom, and the Soviet Union emerging as the most powerful among them. Once more, an effort was made to create a global organization, one that might succeed where the League of Nations had failed: as a peacekeeper. This organization was (and is) the United Nations, headquartered in New York City.

The scope of the UN has grown vastly in the decades since the organization's founding, and it now helps to address and provide support in a broad array of fields, including many aspects of culture, society, and health. Its primary responsibility, however, remains its peacekeeping role. At the heart of this function is the UN Security Council, with five permanent members—the United States, China, France, England, and the Russian Republic (formerly the Soviet Union)—along with ten other rotating seats. The United Nations Charter makes the Security Council's authority clear, stating that it has the "primary responsibility for the maintenance of international peace and security" and that "the Members of the United Nations agree to accept and carry out the decisions of the Security Council in accordance with the present Charter."

International Power Struggles

By the mid-1950s, the balance of power had shifted once again. Britain and France had lost much of their global influence, in part because many of their colonial lands had achieved independence. The two most powerful nations remaining, the Soviet Union and the United States, became the world's sole superpowers, as they were called, and would remain so for the next four decades.

Partners during World War II against Germany, the American and the Soviet governments now became enemies as the differences between their political structures (democratic/capitalist vs. communist/socialist, respectively) generated increasing friction. As other countries allied themselves with one or the other side, a bitter contest known as the Cold War emerged. In his book *Overthrow*, journalist Stephen Kinzler describes one aspect of this friction: "The United States was gripped by a fear of encirclement, a terrible sense that it was losing the postwar battle of ideologies."

US-Soviet tensions continued to mount through the 1950s and 1960s. Many leaders and citizens on both sides were convinced that they were in grave danger of domination by the country half a world away. The most dramatic result of this was an arms race: a massive buildup of weapons, both conventional and nuclear. At the same time, both superpowers sought to extend their influence in the rest of the world. This policy often was pursued by means of espionage and the establishment of military bases, but it also took the form of supporting factions in regional or civil wars by providing money, personnel, weapons, and other aid.

One of the most crucial of these struggles was the Korean War of the early 1950s. It was the first of the large-scale armed interventions of the Cold War. The hostilities in Korea allowed

An American infantry tank stationed near Masan, South Korea, defends the zone against North Korean troops on August 16, 1950.

the two superpowers to indirectly express aggression toward each other, waging war by proxy in a small region far from their own borders.

The Korean War

On one side, in the southern part of the Korean peninsula, was the Republic of Korea. Its opponent was the Democratic People's Republic of Korea to the north. This division, which had been arbitrarily imposed on Korea, was the direct cause of the conflict between the north and the south. Korea had been annexed by

Japan in 1910, but with the defeat of Japan during World War II in 1945, control passed to the victorious Allies. The country was then split along the 38th parallel, and in what was intended to be a temporary administrative measure, United States troops occupied South Korea and Soviet troops took up position in the north.

The situation, tense from the start, escalated into open warfare when North Korean forces, supported by the communist People's Republic of China and the Soviet Union, attacked the south in June 1950. At that point, the UN authorized the United States and South Korea to conduct military action to repel the invaders. This armed conflict ended with an armistice that was signed in 1953.

The peace agreement restored the original post–World War II border between the antagonists and created a demilitarized zone between them as a buffer. Part of the cease-fire agreement called for the United States to maintain a military presence in South Korea.

The conflict in Korea proved to be a key element in deciding the future of the Cold War. It contributed to the huge buildup of weaponry that characterized the era, overseen by what became known as the "military-industrial complex." This phrase—referring to the close alliance between government military forces and the private defense industry—was coined by President Dwight D. Eisenhower. A hero of World War II, Eisenhower began his first term in office in 1953, just as the Korean peace treaty was signed.

Conflict in Southeast Asia

Prior to World War II, Vietnam had been part of French Indochina, a colonized region that also included modern-day Cambodia and Laos. In the last months of the war, Japan ousted the French from the area. When Japan surrendered in 1945, the French briefly reoccupied Indochina, but the long-term status of that part of Southeast Asia was uncertain.

Shortly after the return of the French, conflict broke out in Vietnam. This was the First Indochina War, also called the French Indochina War. Vietnamese rebels, demanding independence, occupied the northern part of the country and declared a socialist government, to be known as the Democratic Republic of Vietnam. In large part because of their work in relieving the effects of wartime famine, the rebels enjoyed strong support from the region's citizens.

As with Korea, regional conflict soon escalated into a full-scale war. It was again an example of war by proxy: French and South Vietnamese forces were on one side, with military and economic aid coming primarily from Britain and the United States; on the other side were the rebels, who waged a guerrilla war with aid from communist nations, notably China and the Soviet Union. The world's two superpowers, the United States and the Soviet Union, were now indirectly battling each other in Vietnam, backing the armies of South and North Vietnam, respectively.

In 1954, an international conference in Geneva brokered a cease-fire and, as part of the peace agreement, Vietnam was divided in two. The French forces withdrew in defeat, and the United States took over military operations in the south. The American authorities considered it their job to maintain a military presence to support the south's pro-Western government. Within a decade, the role of the US military would be very different.

A Buildup of Armed Forces

The North Vietnamese continued to wage a guerrilla war as an estimated one million people relocated, mostly from the north to the south. American military advisors remained in South Vietnam, although there was little major military action. Then, in 1964, American authorities decided to step up the country's armed presence in the region.

The Military-Industrial Complex

In his "Farewell Address to the Nation," delivered when he stepped down in 1961, President Dwight D. Eisenhower touched on several aspects of the United States' role in world politics and defense. He expressed his belief that the United States had a responsibility to meet all future challenges, but he also noted how easy it would be for the defense industry to take control of an already-escalating arms race:

> Crises there will continue to be. In meeting them, whether foreign or domestic, great or small, there is a recurring temptation to feel that some spectacular and costly action could become the miraculous solution to all current difficulties … [However,] we must guard against the acquisition of unwarranted influence, whether sought or unsought, by the military-industrial complex. The potential for the disastrous rise of misplaced power exists and will persist. We must never let the weight of this combination endanger our liberties or democratic processes.

During the 1960s, many countries allied themselves with one or the other side of the Cold War. Some did so willingly. Others resisted alignment and, as a result, were sometimes the targets of armed intervention.

As the Cold War ground on, the United States allocated ever-increasing funds to its military forces. This continued to provide business for the US defense industry. Uncertain international conditions also gave the nation's leaders justification for deploying forces around the world in the name of anticommunist action. Troops were sent to Eastern Europe, the Middle East, South America, and Southeast Asia. South Vietnam would become the site of a long, costly, and controversial military intervention.

The trigger for this new policy came in the summer of 1964, when US president Lyndon B. Johnson announced that North Vietnamese patrol boats had illegally attacked American ships in international waters in the Gulf of Tonkin. The report of one of these incidents was later shown to have had, at best, questionable validity. Nonetheless, Johnson used the episode to urge increased US military intervention. Congress agreed and granted the authority to openly engage in military activities, thereby unofficially declaring war.

Johnson's justification for encouraging this action by Congress was the belief that it was a necessary step in the face of a continuing threat from the Soviets and the Chinese. If it were not taken, he argued, all of Vietnam would come under communist influence, followed by Vietnam's neighboring countries. The United States hoped to contain the expansion of Soviet and Chinese influence by avoiding a so-called domino effect, in which one nation after another "falls" to communism as a result of the first nation's adoption of that political system.

The result of the congressional action was a quick and massive buildup of US forces in the south, along with a campaign of incursions including bombing and search-and-destroy missions. In retaliation, North Vietnam tenaciously fought back with a combination of conventional forces (mostly in the north) and guerrilla armies (mostly in the south). By 1968, there were more than five hundred thousand US troops in Vietnam, with still more on the way. This buildup continued despite large-scale casualties and no clear signs of victory or even an imminent cease-fire.

Seeking an End to the Vietnam War

Meanwhile, the news coming from the battlegrounds in Southeast Asia—in particular, the daily television news showing graphic war scenes—had a polarizing effect. Massive antiwar protests

American marines, aided by a tank and a CH-46 helicopter, carry out a reconnaissance mission in a Vietnamese jungle on April 20, 1967.

were held around the world as many insisted that Vietnam had become a quagmire—a metaphorical swamp from which there was no clear or easy escape.

When Richard Nixon succeeded Johnson as president in 1969, the armed intervention and occupation in Vietnam continued on a large scale, despite the fact that Nixon had promised to cede primary control to the South Vietnamese armed forces. After several more years of bloody conflict, including illegal US bombings of neighboring Cambodia and Laos, huge losses on both sides, and intense diplomatic negotiations, a tentative cease-fire was brokered.

In light of this, and despite continuing violence, US forces began to withdraw from South Vietnam in 1970 and 1971. By the summer of 1972, all US ground forces were gone from the region. However, air strikes by US planes continued into late 1972.

The overall US military, civilian, and diplomatic presence in Vietnam continued to decrease, and the withdrawal was completed in 1975. The subsequent occupation by North Vietnamese forces of Saigon, South Vietnam's capital city (now part of the Greater Ho Chi Minh City metropolitan area), marked the reunification of the country—and the end of what had been the most deeply unpopular military intervention by the United States on foreign soil to date. It also marked the beginning of a period during which the United States significantly reassessed its need to conduct armed intervention.

Many observers asserted that future large-scale interventions would require widespread approval by a majority of US citizens if they were to fully succeed. Furthermore, they argued, popular approval would be forthcoming only if intervention were deemed clearly necessary for survival. According to the report of a congressional committee in 1975, "Perhaps the most pointed lesson US leaders learned in Vietnam was that national decisions, however desirable they may otherwise seem, must be acceptable to the people. No great problems would surface if US survival were not at stake and the public knew it."

Soviet Intervention in Afghanistan

The lingering effects of the Vietnam War are still being felt today throughout the world, and its lessons are still being absorbed. However, that conflict in Southeast Asia was by no means the last major event of the twentieth century to affect future thinking about global intervention.

Although collapse of the Soviet Union was complete by the early 1990s, its roots stretched back into the late 1970s. The causes of this collapse were varied. One was a growing acknowledgment of the shortcomings of the political structure of the USSR. As a result, there had been a dramatic increase in demands, both from inside and outside the Soviet Union, for greater personal freedoms and economic reforms.

Another important factor in the Soviet collapse was a failed military intervention: the ruinous, decade-long incursion into Afghanistan. This unsuccessful Soviet military venture has frequently been compared to the American experience in Vietnam.

The Soviet Union first intervened militarily in Afghanistan to back the government of what was then the Democratic Republic of Afghanistan, a communist regime closely allied with the Soviets. Opposing this authority was an amalgamation of mujahideen (an Arabic term for warriors or independence fighters) who sought to gain control of Afghanistan for an Islamic regime. At this point, the Afghan mujahideen were supported by a coalition including the United States, England, and Pakistan, as part of those countries' continuing policy to contain communist expansion.

Late in 1979, at the request of Afghanistan's rulers, the Soviet Union dramatically stepped up its military presence in the country. It attacked the rebel-held capital city of Kabul and claimed victory for the Democratic Republic. The move outraged many predominantly Muslim nations around the world, and the UN General Assembly also voiced a protest.

It was later revealed that the United States had taken an active part in encouraging a Soviet incursion into Afghanistan by supplying nonlethal aid to the mujahideen. The goal of this tactic was to draw Moscow into a military quagmire not unlike what the United States had experienced in Vietnam. In 1998, Zbigniew Brzezinski, former national security adviser to US president Jimmy Carter, admitted, "We didn't push the Russians to intervene,

A Soviet tank travels through the Afghan countryside in 1979 as part of a military intervention in Afghanistan.

but we knowingly increased the probability that they would."

At least partly because of this, the Soviet Union established a long-term presence in Afghanistan, and the Soviet military largely succeeded in controlling the country's cities. Elsewhere, however, rebel forces continued to control the vast, rugged, sparsely populated Afghan deserts and mountains—by far the largest part of the disputed region.

The Soviets made a number of unsuccessful incursions into the countryside, and after a decade, they acknowledged their failure. They began to withdraw forces in 1985, gradually transferring power and authority to Afghan individuals and institutions. Meanwhile, the United States and its allies stepped up their aid to the rebels. By 1989, Soviet forces were gone from the country.

The USSR Collapses

The Soviet Union began to seriously unravel in 1990. The deep changes during this period, spurred in part by the Soviet public's weariness with the long and unsuccessful occupation of Afghanistan, were symbolized by a single occurrence: the destruction of the Berlin Wall. This infamous concrete barrier had been erected by Soviet-aligned East Germany in 1961.

The Berlin Wall separated the Western-allied portion of the city from the rest of Berlin, which was then completely surrounded by East Germany. The wall's twofold purpose was to prevent East Germans from defecting to the West and to control other movement across the border.

For decades after the wall went up, Western nations, in particular the United States, called for it to be dismantled. By the mid-1980s, the movement to bring down the wall had reached its zenith. In June 1987, US president Ronald Reagan gave a speech at Berlin's Brandenburg Gate, one of the city's most famous landmarks. He challenged his counterpart in the Soviet Union, Mikhail Gorbachev, using the now-famous words, "Mr. Gorbachev, open this gate! Mr. Gorbachev, tear down this wall!"

Massive protest movements around the world over the next months encouraged the citizens of Berlin to take action, and over the winter and spring of 1989–1990 they began to remove small parts of the wall. By the early summer of 1990, the East German government acquiesced. In June, it ordered its soldiers to dismantle the last of the wall.

The immediate consequence of the destruction of this widely despised barrier was the reunification of East and West Germany. However, it was also a powerful emblem signaling a much broader turn of events: the demise of communism in virtually all of the Eastern European nations that had been part of the Soviet Union.

Emboldened by the events in Germany, smaller states within the Soviet sphere of influence, including Georgia, Lithuania, and Estonia, began to break away and assert their independence. These nations banded together in a loose commonwealth, and the Soviet Union itself dissolved in 1991. Only a handful of nations with communist leadership remained. As the USSR split into many small republics, the United States became the world's only superpower, and the Cold War ended.

Again and again, military intervention during the twentieth century led to increased violence and shifts in power between the world's most powerful nations. Sometimes, these efforts were successful in preventing further violence and protecting the powerless, as in the case of the United States' intervention in World War II, which helped bring an end to the most devastating conflict the world has ever seen. Other times, however, these interventions produced unwanted consequences for the nations that instigated them. While all nations hoped for peace, there remained many cases in which world powers considered armed intervention justified and necessary.

Chapter Two

REASONS FOR MILITARY INTERVENTION

Nations justify their armed intervention on foreign soil in a variety of ways. They argue that a balance of power must be maintained, insist that their national security is at risk, or contend that they have a responsibility to step in when a humanitarian crisis is underway. Many interventions are motivated by a nation's potential for economic gain.

However, the justifications that countries offer up for their actions can be highly subjective. In cases where some see the use of force as necessary, others may view it as unjust or even criminal. Countless variables—among them confusion, miscommunication, misperception, intolerance, and sometimes greed and the desire to expand territory—can further muddy a situation.

Opposite: The founding conference of the United Nations, an organization founded to seek peaceful solutions to global conflict, takes place in San Francisco in 1945.

Historians are constantly revising their opinions and interpretations of past events. The lessons a given generation or group draws from history can be dramatically different from those drawn by another generation or perspective. In short, affairs among nations are relative and cannot be seen in black and white. In the words of British political science and international affairs professors Michael Cox and Caroline Kennedy-Pipe, history is not comprised of "morality tales in which heroes and evil demons are locked in mortal combat."

Intervention for Economic Gain

One reason for considering armed intervention would be to ensure a nation's survival in the face of hostile attack. However, such cases of basic survival are extreme examples and occur relatively rarely. There are other, more common reasons for a nation to launch a military intervention. One of these is to protect or increase its own economic well-being.

A nation's use of armed intervention to protect its economic interests is a well-established principle. It is generally understood and agreed upon that nations have legal and moral rights to intervene if their own resources are in danger. The primary UN document addressing this principle, the United Nations Charter of Economic Rights and Duties, is explicit in its approval of the right of a nation to not only assert its sovereignty (independent statehood), but also to maintain its basic economic structures. The charter specifies that every country has the right to "full permanent sovereignty including possession, use, and disposal, over its wealth, natural resources, and economic activities."

However, laws and morality become murkier when expansionism, colonialism, or economic gain is involved. Interventions for these reasons are widespread and have occurred frequently throughout history. One example of a nation instigating armed intervention for economic purposes involves the need to secure ample supplies of oil.

The question of sufficient oil supplies has been a major factor since the dawn of the Industrial Revolution in the nineteenth century. The explosion in the use of machinery for manufacturing during this time, and later the advent of the automobile, made oil an essential component in the economic health of virtually every developed nation in the world. This is true today even for countries with large populations of very poor people: without sufficient resources of oil, a nation's prosperity—and therefore its ability to maintain political stability and strength—is likely to collapse.

This is as true for the United States as for any other developed or developing nation. Despite large domestic oil supplies to draw from, total US consumption is far greater than the country's own resources (and far greater than the consumption of other nations, as well). As a result, much of the oil consumed in the United States comes from overseas. (Again, the United States is not the only country that relies on foreign oil. The need for oil imports is even more significant in industrialized countries that lack sufficient resources of their own, such as Japan.)

A significant percentage of US oil imports comes from the nations of the Middle East. On numerous occasions over the years, the volatile political situation in that region has put US oil interests there in jeopardy. As a result, the threat or actual use of armed intervention has been a major factor in American relations with the nations of the Middle East for decades.

The 1970s Oil Embargo

The United States faced a crisis in the mid-1970s when the oil-rich nations of the Middle East and their partners in OPEC, the Organization of Petroleum Exporting Countries, imposed an oil embargo. (An embargo is a block on trade.) This was a reaction to the continuing support that the United States and its allies offered to Israel, a nation whose existence has always been bitterly opposed by the Arab world. The trigger for the oil crisis of the 1970s was the Arab-Israeli conflict known as the Yom Kippur War. During this war, the United States provided Israel with limited amounts of weapons and other supplies; at the same time, the Soviet Union aided the Arab nations of Syria and Egypt in similar ways.

When the oil-producing nations imposed their embargo in late 1973, the effects on industrialized nations everywhere were immediate. The price of oil quadrupled, and manufacturing powerhouses such as the United States were hard hit. The embargo had significant effects on the daily life of Americans as well. US motorists waited in long lines at service stations to buy gasoline, which had become scarce. A more serious, life-threatening aspect of the crisis was that many people had difficulty finding enough heating oil to stay warm in the winter. Worldwide, there was widespread discontent, as well as the potential for global bankruptcy and recession. The most vulnerable nations faced the threat of economic meltdowns, and some analysts even suggested that entire political systems might collapse.

The administration of US president Richard Nixon instigated formal talks with the oil-producing nations. The goal was twofold: to lift the embargo and to persuade Israel to appease Arab states by withdrawing from disputed territories. These talks proved successful on both fronts, and the embargo ended in the spring of 1974.

However, the embargo had a long-term effect: it created a major shift in political relations worldwide. Many countries altered their positions from being strongly pro-Israel to a posture that was less threatening to Arab nations. For example, the United Kingdom refused to let US forces use British military bases in England and its territory in Cyprus to airlift supplies to Israel.

Worldwide fuel shortages resulted from an oil embargo by the Organization of Petroleum Exporting Countries (OPEC). Here, drivers line up to wait for fuel circa 1974.

Since the United States never wavered in its support for Israel, such policy shifts strained US diplomatic relationships with those nations that had changed their positions.

Operation Desert Storm

For decades, Western military intervention in the Middle East remained a possibility. However, it did not become a reality until the start of the first Gulf War, also called the Persian Gulf War, in 1990–1991. This war was triggered by the invasion of the nation of Kuwait by neighboring Iraq. The ensuing response, by a coalition of nations led by the United States, was the first

Diplomacy or Force?

In the wake of an oil embargo that began in 1973, US authorities seriously considered armed intervention as a solution if, in the future, diplomacy failed to avert a crisis that could affect economic stability in the United States. Numerous studies examined the effects of a potential intervention in an oil-supplying region. One such study was summed up in 1975 in a report to the US Congress. The report stated:

> Successful operations would be assured only if this country could satisfy all aspects of a five-part mission:
> - Seize required oil installations intact.
> - Secure them for weeks, months, or years.
> - Restore wrecked assets rapidly.
> - Operate all installations without the owner's assistance.
> - Guarantee safe overseas passage for supplies and petroleum products.

That same year, US secretary of state Henry Kissinger told *Business Week* magazine that military intervention against oil-producing nations would be "a very dangerous course" but did not rule out the possibility. "I am not saying that there is no circumstance where we would not use force. But it is one thing to use it in the case of a dispute over price; it's another where there's some actual strangulation of the industrial world."

A number of governments, including those of the Soviet Union, Egypt, and Algeria, condemned Kissinger's assertions. However, other leaders and policy experts defended his statements, citing the UN's assertion of a nation's right to use force if and when its survival, or that of its allies, is at stake.

military intervention undertaken by American troops after the collapse of the Soviet Union, so it gave the United States a chance to flex its new status as the world's only surviving superpower.

The roots of the Iraqi-Kuwaiti conflict extended back many years. More immediately, in the wake of a costly war with Iran, Iraq's dictator, Saddam Hussein, desperately needed to refill his treasury with oil revenues. He owed billions of dollars to Kuwait, which had lent Iraq funds to finance the war with Iran. Annexing Kuwait by force would have given him access to that country's huge stockpile of oil, allowing him to gain a large stretch of coastline vital for increased trade, and, of course, negating the debt.

Hussein used several questionable reasons to justify his incursion into Kuwait. For starters, he accused Kuwait of illegally drilling to obtain Iraqi oil. He also cited a historical reason: the division of what was then a British-controlled territory into smaller countries in 1913—an act that had made Kuwait a separate nation. Hussein argued that this division had been illegal and used it to assert his claim that Kuwait was rightfully part of Iraq.

So, in the summer of 1990, Iraqi forces moved into Kuwait and quickly took control. The UN passed numerous resolutions condemning the occupation, as well as a series of economic sanctions (penalties) against Iraq. Attempts were made to begin diplomatic discussions over the issue. However, these talks were unsatisfactory and were soon abandoned.

The UN then gave approval to begin Operation Desert Storm, the name given to a military intervention undertaken by a coalition force of thirty-four nations. The United States spearheaded this action under the direction of the administration of President George H. W. Bush, with significant military and economic help from its allies, notably Egypt, Saudi Arabia, and the United Kingdom.

The US government offered several justifications for the intervention. Among these were the need to stabilize the situation and minimize casualties; to counter Saddam Hussein's dictatorial regime, which was accused of harboring anti-American terrorists; to promote democracy in the region; and to protect US access to oil supplies.

Saddam Hussein managed to occupy Kuwait for seven months before accepting a cease-fire. When the hostilities ended, Iraqi forces withdrew from Kuwait. However, Hussein remained in power, which led to severe criticism of President Bush, both in America and around the world.

Intervention to Protect National Security

Armed intervention is often employed in order to protect national or international security. The most notable modern instances of this have been the US invasions and subsequent occupations of Afghanistan and Iraq.

In October 2001, in the wake of the September 11 terrorist attacks, the administration of President George W. Bush (son of the first President Bush) launched a military intervention in Afghanistan. This incursion was carried out with aid from the United Kingdom. It was designed to eliminate the safe haven that existed in Afghanistan for al-Qaeda terrorists, particularly their leader, Osama bin Laden. This safe haven, Bush argued, was a clear threat to the national security of the United States.

After the initial attacks, US forces remained in Afghanistan to continue the search for bin Laden and other terrorist leaders. However, the focus of US military power soon shifted back to Iraq, which in 2003 faced the incursion of another coalition led by the United States. This conflict became known variously as the second Gulf War, Operation Iraqi Freedom, or simply the Iraq War.

Dozens of aircraft like this B-52 Stratofortress heavy bomber launched air and missile strikes in Afghanistan on October 7, 2001.

As he had in Afghanistan, President Bush justified the renewed US incursion into Iraq on the grounds of national security. The most important reason he cited involved intelligence reports that Saddam Hussein was secretly in possession of heavy ordnance, commonly referred to as "weapons of mass destruction," or WMDs. The presence of the weapons could not be confirmed or denied by international inspectors, however, and strong evidence later surfaced that Bush's intelligence had been incorrect.

President Bush was unable to garner widespread international support for the second invasion. Indeed, the United States came under intense criticism around the world for its venture into Iraq. Only a few world politicians openly supported Bush in this case, the most notable being British prime minister Tony Blair. Nonetheless, Bush and his advisers pursued their course, which led to a massive US presence in Iraq and the eventual capture and execution of Saddam Hussein.

Intervention for Political Reasons

Still another reason for the use of armed intervention, in addition to those involving questions of economics and security, is the perceived need to engineer the replacement of leadership of other nations—that is, a regime change. This is often done in order to install leaders and political systems more in line with the policies and political goals of the intervening nation.

Clearly, regime change is closely intertwined with other reasons for intervention. Iraq is a good example of this. The second Bush administration gave a variety of justifications for the Iraq War aside from the possible presence of WMDs in the country. It also cited well-documented and ongoing instances of domestic repression and violence, Hussein's harboring of terrorists, and his overtly hostile attitude toward Israel. These additional reasons were necessary because the suspicion that Iraq possessed WMDs wasn't sufficient justification for mounting an armed incursion. Political science professor Michael Walzer explains how the Bush administration used these additional factors to justify the intervention:

[A]ll the reasons suggested the need, this time, to march on Baghdad and replace the ... regime. But the fact that France (say) possessed weapons of mass destruction was never imagined as an occasion for war. It was the character of its regime that made Iraq dangerous: the US government claimed that Saddam's was an inherently aggressive and an inherently murderous regime ... What had happened before would happen again unless the regime was replaced.

Ousting a Panamanian Leader

Iraq is not the only country where the United States has brought about a regime change. The United States intervened in the Central American nation of Panama in 1989 to depose a hostile dictator, Manuel Noriega.

President George H. W. Bush used four reasons to justify the incursion, which was code-named Operation Just Cause. He cited the need for safeguarding the lives of US citizens in Panama, asserting that Noriega had declared a state of war with the United States that threatened the lives of the approximately thirty-five thousand Americans there. He also offered up other goals for the intervention: promoting democracy and human rights in Panama; reducing the extensive drug trafficking that Noriega's government had condoned; and supporting and protecting America's interest in the Panama Canal, a shipping lane that has long been a vital part of US economic well-being. Even though the United States had agreed to hand over the canal by January 1, 1990, Noriega's annulment of elections the previous spring gave Bush justification for a full-scale invasion involving some twenty-five thousand American troops.

Regime change typically involves swapping one leader for another. In this case, however, the goal was primarily to remove Noriega. "Operation Just Cause was a new departure:

US troops land in Panama on May 23, 1989, as part of an incursion called Operation Just Cause.

disproportionate force used unilaterally to overthrow, rather than install, a dictator," explains historian Niall Ferguson.

The invasion of Panama was successful from the standpoint of the United States. Noriega was captured and deemed a prisoner of war. Later tried in a court in Miami, the former strongman was convicted of drug trafficking, racketeering, and money laundering. In April 2010, Noriega was extradited to France, and there, on July 7, 2010, he was sentenced to seven years in prison for money laundering. In 2011, he was extradited back to Panama, where he had been convicted in absentia (without being present at the trial) of murder, embezzlement, and corruption—crimes committed during his time as leader of Panama in the 1980s. He died in 2017.

Some polls at the time of Noriega's capture indicated that a majority of Americans and Panamanians approved of Operation Just Cause. However, the governments and citizens of many other nations were outraged, arguing that the United States had committed an unlawful act of aggression. The UN General Assembly voted overwhelmingly to condemn the invasion, although that body's Security Council stopped short of passing a formal resolution demanding that US troops return home. A coalition of Western Hemisphere nations, the Organization of American States, went further and called for the withdrawal of US troops.

Critics of such actions charge that, among other things, coercive regime change is not sufficient justification for invasion. These critics assert that armed incursions such as the one into Panama are, essentially, acts of imperialism—that is, the acquisition or control of a country by another, more powerful country. Not everyone agrees with this, however. For example, in an essay for the *Stanford Encyclopedia of Philosophy*, Brian Orend, a Canadian professor of ethics, writes:

In my view, forcible post-war regime change can be permissible provided: 1) the war itself was just and conducted properly; 2) the target regime was illegitimate, thus forfeiting its state rights; 3) the goal of the reconstruction is a minimally just regime; and 4) respect for jus in bello *[just war] and human rights is integral to the transformation process itself. The permission is then granted because the transformation: 1) violates neither state nor human rights; 2) its expected consequences are very desirable, namely, satisfied human rights for the local population and increased international peace and security for everyone; and 3) the post-war moment is especially promising regarding the possibilities for reform. And the transformation will be successful when there's: 1) a stable new regime; 2) run entirely by locals; which is 3) minimally just.*

Intervention in Matters of Statehood and Independence

Yet another common rationalization for military intervention is that it responds to attempts by breakaway states to declare independence from a larger nation. A familiar example is the American Revolutionary War, which was the result of the settlers' resistance to England's efforts to retain control of its North American colonies.

There have been many other examples over the centuries. One instance arose after the collapse of the Soviet Union in 1991. The state of Chechnya, in the southwest corner of the former Soviet Union, renamed itself the Chechen Republic and declared itself independent. Russian forces, which were moved into the area to prevent Chechnya from seceding, then engaged the Chechen rebels in an ongoing battle. Officially, the Russian forces withdrew from the region in 2009, after nearly two decades and tens of thousands of deaths; however, sporadic violence continues.

Much of the violence over the issue of Chechen independence is interwoven with ethnic conflict, and such clashes between rival ethnic groups are often a primary reason for military intervention elsewhere as well. At any given time, several violent ethnic or nationalist conflicts have raged in locations around the globe. Ethnic conflict can occur across borders, of course, but it is also found between factions within a nation. In the latter case, ethnic conflict can become the motivating trigger for armed intervention in the name of humanitarian reasons, to put an end to violence or widespread human rights violations.

Intervention for Humanitarian Reasons

A prominent example of armed intervention for a humanitarian cause is the action the North Atlantic Treaty Organization (NATO) took in 1999 to stop a campaign of ethnic cleansing in the eastern European region of Kosovo, a self-declared independent part of what was then Yugoslavia. Kosovo's experience with ethnic cleansing—widespread instances of murder, torture, mass sexual assault, and other crimes against humanity—came in the aftermath of the Bosnian War of the mid-1990s, a conflict largely conducted along ethnic lines.

The Bosnian War resulted in massive forced relocations from Kosovo of ethnic Albanians—800,000 to one million, according to reliable estimates—and some 11,000 deaths. In 1999, NATO forces responded by bombing Yugoslavia in a successful bid to force Slobodan Milosevic, the president of Yugoslavia, to withdraw his forces from Kosovo. Milošević and several other Serbian and Yugoslavian leaders were subsequently placed on trial for war crimes. (Milosevic died in 2006 before his trial concluded.)

Another example of armed intervention in a humanitarian crisis came in 2014, when US president Barack Obama authorized airstrikes against the extremist Islamic State in Iraq and Syria, or ISIS, as it committed horrendous crimes against the Yazidi people, a religious minority in Iraq. These airstrikes were limited but many agree they helped hundreds or even thousands of Yazidis escape.

There are perhaps as many reasons for armed intervention as there are conflicts in the world. Likewise, there are many ways to carry out such incursions, and the methods employed can be instrumental in the success or failure of a mission. Weighing the reasons for stepping in against the reasons for respecting national sovereignty is no easy task, and it remains a matter of often-impassioned debate.

Chapter Three

ALTERNATIVES TO ARMED INTERVENTION

Most nations consider military intervention a last resort. The costs of such intervention are high: it requires a massive investment of governmental resources and funds and can at times lead to hundreds or even thousands of casualties. It is reasonable, then, that nonmilitary solutions are often favored by the international community and by most nations connected with any given conflict.

Fortunately, governments have several alternatives to deploying military force. For these options to be feasible, however, the leaders of all the countries potentially involved must be acting in good faith and must be willing and able to exercise nonmilitary options before more drastic measures become advisable.

Opposite: An estimated six thousand children, including these boys in 2016, are registered at a United Nations Children's Fund (UNICEF) school in a refugee camp in Iraq.

Governments have several ways of resolving disputes without resorting to force. These include diplomacy and mediation (negotiations held with the help of a disinterested third party); legal appeals to international courts; economic sanctions; and nonviolent peacekeeping or humanitarian missions (for example, to protect a threatened nation or ethnic group). Espionage, though secretive and invasive, might also be considered a nonmilitary method of avoiding overt warfare.

Diplomacy

On the subject of international relations, Carl von Clausewitz, a German military theorist of the nineteenth century, commented: "War is not merely a political act, but also a political instrument … a carrying out of the same [intent] by other means." However, it is generally agreed that in most cases the first and best method of conflict resolution is not Clausewitz's aggressive "other means," but diplomacy. International diplomacy involves civilized, formal political discussions and agreements among countries. Historically, it has been an extremely effective method, used to prevent armed conflict on countless occasions.

Nations typically establish diplomatic relationships by maintaining representative embassies in one another's countries. These embassies are staffed by professional diplomats and ambassadors, who are aided by other governmental officials as needed. In the US system, the State Department is the branch of government with primary responsibility for official diplomatic duties. (In other countries, the departments of state have different names. For example, the equivalent branch of government in England is called the Foreign and Commonwealth Office, typically shortened to "the Foreign Office.")

Diplomacy is not always carried out by the career diplomats of the State Department. Sometimes, informal representatives are asked to carry out international missions. For example, a number of former US presidents, notably Jimmy Carter, have prominently fulfilled these roles after leaving office.

Either way, the expectation is that mutually acceptable solutions to a problem can be reached through detailed, extensive discussions. Diplomatic discussions typically cover such topics as peace negotiations, cultural exchanges, border and ethnic disputes, and environmental and economic concerns. Diplomacy is particularly important to small states, which often lack extensive military resources or enough economic influence to secure their goals in the arena of world politics.

Diplomacy Under President Obama

Under the administration of President Barack Obama, the nation's chief diplomat was, for a time, Secretary of State Hillary Clinton. The Obama administration's overall policy was to mitigate the hard-line foreign policies of the previous administration. George W. Bush and his advisers established a more aggressive foreign policy than had been typical in the late twentieth century. Many critics believed that the choice to downplay diplomatic routes in favor of a more belligerent approach had the effect of damaging the international reputation of the United States and destroying much of the goodwill the country had enjoyed.

In contrast, Obama's strategy was to advocate an increase in the nation's diplomatic presence, particularly in challenging situations such as those with Iraq, Iran, Russia, Pakistan, and China. This emphasis on diplomacy was seen by the Obama administration as a way to boost the nation's damaged standing. Soon after her appointment, Clinton began to publicly assert her opinion that Obama's policy was being well received in other countries. Early in 2009, she told reporters, "We have a lot of damage to repair … In areas of the world that have felt either overlooked, or not receiving appropriate attention for the problems

On July 20, 2015, the United Nations Security Council votes on a nuclear agreement with Iran, brokered by the Obama administration.

they are experiencing, there's a welcoming of the [increased diplomatic] engagement that we are promising."

This new emphasis in America's international diplomatic efforts had another goal beyond improving relations with other countries. It also represented a US intent to play a more prominent role in brokering agreements among other nations. For example, late in 2009, former president Bill Clinton intervened in discussions held in Switzerland involving Turkey and Armenia, two countries with long-standing animosity toward each other, stemming from genocidal attacks on Armenians during World War I. Thanks in part to diplomatic help from the United States, the talks resulted in the establishment of formal relations, and the opening of the border, between these two longtime antagonists.

Diplomacy Under President Trump

The beginning of Donald Trump's presidency in 2017 heralded a significant shift in the nation's policies on diplomacy and a return to a more hard-line approach. His style of diplomacy has been called "unconventional," "unorthodox," and "combative," and has at times alienated many of the United States' closest allies while courting some of its greatest adversaries. Trump and his supporters insist that his tough stance is necessary in order to protect US interests and "put America first."

President Trump has butted heads with US allies on various occasions. For instance, he has expressed opposition to the amount of financial support that the United States has provided to its allies for military defense. He criticized members of the North Atlantic Treaty Organization on July 11, 2018, for being "delinquent" in their spending on defense and urged them to increase that spending right away. After Trump's comments, US Senate Foreign Relations chairman Bob Corker said the president seemed to be trying to "punch our friends in the nose." Nicholas Burns, former ambassador and professor at the Harvard Kennedy School of Government, declared that Trump had launched "diplomatic warfare with America's closest allies." Similarly, Trump pushed allies in Asia to increase their defense spending and "encouraged Japan to buy more American weapons," according to CNN.

Meanwhile, Trump has praised President Vladimir Putin of Russia despite longstanding tensions with that nation over alleged human rights violations and other concerns, and despite widespread agreement within the US intelligence community that Russia conspired to influence the 2016 US presidential election. Trump also became the first US president to meet with Kim Jong Un, the leader of North Korea, one of the United States' longest-standing adversaries, which for years has been working to build a nuclear arsenal and threatening to use those weapons against the United States. This meeting came after heated verbal confrontations with Kim in which Trump pointed to the nuclear firepower of the United States as a potential response to North Korean threats, statements that worried many Americans.

In October 2018, Trump threatened to increase the United States' nuclear arsenal and pull out of the Intermediate-Range

Nuclear Forces Treaty (INF)—an action that would mark a stark reversal from post–Cold War policy. Under the INF, nations with nuclear capability have significantly reduced their stockpiles of nuclear weapons, with almost three thousand missiles destroyed since 1987. Trump accused Russia of failing to follow the terms of the treaty. Speaking of his threat to withdraw, Trump said, "It's a threat to whoever you want," calling out Russia and China specifically. Many leaders on the international stage expressed concern over Trump's statement.

The Trump administration has, in general, seemed to prioritize military spending over diplomacy. The State Department, which is charged with diplomatic duties, has seen massive budget cuts while military defense spending has seen significant increases since Trump's presidency began. Shortly after Trump took office, he fired every foreign ambassador for the United States, with no plans about how to replace many of them. More than one hundred senior foreign service officers left the State Department in his first year, and as of early November 2018, the United States lacked an ambassador to eighteen countries, while dozens of US embassies were reportedly understaffed and almost half of all senior-level positions in the State Department remained vacant.

The road to diplomacy has also been made more difficult by the fact that President Trump has broken several agreements that previous administrations reached with the international community. On May 8, 2018, Trump announced that he would withdraw from a deal with Iran, brokered during the Obama administration, by which Iran agreed to curb its nuclear program in exchange for an end to sanctions. The deal had brought resolution to a decade of conflict between Iran and the international community. Trump also pulled out of the Paris Climate Agreement, an accord between 195 nations designed to combat global warming.

Meanwhile, Trump increased tariffs on products imported to the United States, sparking a trade war with China and boosting tensions between the two nations.

Legal Avenues to Peace

Related to the practice of diplomacy is the use of legal methods as an alternative to military intervention. Perhaps the most common of these legal avenues is to appeal to the UN's International Court of Justice, also known as the World Court. Based in The Hague, in the Netherlands, this entity is composed of fifteen judges, chosen in rotation from among UN member nations.

The World Court is authorized to settle legal disputes among nations and international organizations. Under the UN Charter, all member nations (currently, there are 192) are automatically subject to the court's laws and binding rulings. Nonmember nations may, in some circumstances, also become parties to these statutes. Other groups— such as corporations,

The International Court of Justice holds public hearings in 2006.

nongovernmental organizations, and individuals—do not participate directly in cases before the World Court, although the judicial body can hear testimony and receive information from such parties.

The World Court's powers fall into two basic categories. One concerns rulings on what are formally called "contentious" topics, in which the court works to resolve issues when two nations cannot agree. For example, in 2010, it helped Costa Rica and Nicaragua resolve a dispute over navigation and fishing rights in the river that separates the two countries. The other category concerns opinions that are issued on what is called an "advisory" basis. Unlike contentious issues, advisory opinions are available only to certain UN bodies and agencies, which argue before the court so that it can decide legal issues that have arisen because of actions by the agencies in question. As the name implies, these opinions are simply recommendations, although they are often followed and are influential in diplomatic talks.

Despite the respect given to the court's rulings and recommendations, there has been no clear, strong, and overarching international agreement on what defines the legal use of force in all cases. Military historians Daniel Rice and John Dehn point out that there are many difficulties inherent in unraveling the legality of military intervention: "Even when armed intervention is morally justified, it may not necessarily be consistent with international law. Although the law often reflects accepted moral standards, it does not always do so perfectly." As a result, the World Court's rulings and advisories are not always honored. An example of an advisory opinion that was not honored was the court's finding in 2004 that the construction of a wall by Israel in and around East Jerusalem was contrary to international law and that Israel should desist. Israel chose not to be governed by the advisory opinion, however, and continued to build the wall.

It occasionally happens, as well, that nations ignore World Court decisions that were meant to be binding. The so-called Iran-Contra affair provides an example. The situation developed in the 1980s when the Reagan administration secretly arranged to facilitate the sale of arms to Iran, in defiance of a stated US trade and arms embargo. Some American officials hoped that profits from the illegal arms sales would allow the Central Intelligence Agency to fund anticommunist forces in Nicaragua in a bid to destabilize and overthrow a revolutionary government there.

When the plan was discovered, the administration defended it as being in keeping with the Monroe Doctrine, a policy that holds that the United States may intervene in the affairs of Latin American countries if it affects US security. However, in a suit brought by Nicaragua, the World Court ruled that the United States had used excessive force. The US government simply ignored both the verdict and related criticism on the home front.

An example of a World Court decision that was accepted by both parties concerns a land dispute between the African nations of Nigeria and Cameroon. After fifteen years of debate and sporadic violence, the court brokered an agreement between these countries concerning control over the Bakassi Peninsula. This peninsula and its offshore deposits are home to between two hundred thousand and three hundred thousand Nigerian citizens, most of them fishers.

In a ceremony in 2008 overseen by politicians, UN officials, and a military presence, the land was formally handed over to Cameroon, ending decades of dispute over the ancestral home of a majority of its current inhabitants. A spokesman for Umaru Yar'Adua, Nigeria's president, commented to reporters, "This handing-over process, as painful as it is for everyone, including the president, is a commitment we have made to the international community, and we have a responsibility to keep it." Savior Nyong, chairman of the Bakassi local government, added that Nigeria was willing to abide by the World Court's decision, although the ruling was not what the country had hoped for. Nyong commented, "Even though there's pain in our hearts and minds, we have fielded the trauma, and we are thankful for a peaceful handover."

Economic Sanctions

If diplomatic and legal actions are unsuccessful in resolving disputes, the usual next step in nonmilitary intervention involves economic sanctions. These penalties, which can be partial or complete, are imposed on a nation (or group of nations) by another nation (or group of nations). Economic sanctions typically include tariffs, trade barriers, import duties, import or export quotas, embargoes, and the freezing of economic assets or the restriction of financial aid. Sanctions can be global (imposed by virtually all nations), multilateral (imposed by more than one nation), or unilateral (imposed by only one nation).

Economic sanctions are often seen as a last resort before military intervention is deemed necessary. Writer and editor Franklin Foer, writing in *Slate*, explains: "Because economic sanctions can strangle an economy, they are considered one step shy of war. Indeed, it has become almost a diplomatic necessity to level sanctions prior to military intervention, to show that all other options have been exhausted."

In their extreme form, economic sanctions are comparable to the ancient practice of siege warfare, in which a military force would surround and isolate a town, denying passage to people and supplies in an effort to subdue the population. Creating shortages of food, water, medicine, and fuel have a dramatic impact on all aspects of community life. In this way, the consequences of economic sanctions can be severe enough to impoverish the affected nation or endanger its survival. Today, however, sanctions rarely reach such a level of extremity.

More commonly, sanctions take the form of a specific restriction called a trade sanction, which is far less serious than a full economic sanction. Trade sanctions most frequently involve one nation removing another from its "preference programs"—that is, basic trade privileges that are routinely extended to friendly

An Iranian man protests sanctions imposed by the international community against his country during a demonstration in 2014.

countries, such as Most Favored Nation trade status or loans from the Export-Import Bank. Although trade sanctions may cause some economic hardships and impede prosperity, they are clearly less disruptive than full sanctions.

The imposition of trade sanctions may be triggered by any number of events, although often the cause is unresolved trade disputes. For example, if one nation believes that another is unfairly subsidizing exports of a product, or unfairly protecting its own trade from overseas competition, it may choose to impose high import duties, or some other penalty, on goods or services from the trading partner. Increased import duties result in decreased profits for those trying to sell their goods, so trade sanctions can be an effective tool of persuasion.

The Increasing Role of Sanctions

Partial and full economic sanctions are being used more and more often. This is because these measures occupy a useful middle ground in international relations. They are generally more substantial and effective than mere diplomatic protests but less problematic and far less costly than military intervention, in both economic and human terms.

The increased use of economic sanctions is evident from the record of the UN, which has the power to use them to address what its charter calls "threats of aggression" and "breaches of peace." In the forty-five years between 1945 and 1990—coinciding with the duration of the Cold War—the body approved full or partial sanctions only twice. However, between 1990 and 2010, the Security Council imposed sanctions twelve times. The nations affected by these decisions included the former Yugoslavia, Libya, Somalia, Liberia, and Haiti. In one notable example, the UN imposed strict sanctions against Iraq in the years after the first Gulf War, in part to encourage the Iraqi government to cooperate with weapons inspectors.

The United States, meanwhile, has imposed sanctions—on its own or in conjunction with other nations—even more often in the recent past. This is in large part possible because of the nation's continuing dominance of the world's economy. In fact, the United States has used the technique far more frequently than any other nation or multinational body in the world, including the UN and the European Union.

Among the nations affected by US economic sanctions in recent years are Iraq, Serbia, Somalia, Libya, Haiti, and Cambodia. Perhaps the best-known instance is the long-standing US embargo against Cuba.

The embargo against Cuba began in 1960, during the Cold War, in the wake of that nation's revolution and in response to its subsequent close alliance with the Soviet Union. US authorities were deeply unwilling to support an antagonistic nation so close to its own borders. Although the United States has come close to easing the embargo at times, for more than five decades virtually no commercial trade with Cuba has been allowed. The Obama administration reestablished diplomatic relations with Cuba, but in 2017 the Trump administration asserted its commitment to restore pre-Obama-era policies toward the island nation.

Do Sanctions Work?

Overall, it can be difficult to make a clear-cut case that sanctions are, or are not, effective. It appears likely that they are only one factor—an important factor, but not the only one—in political change. For example, sanctions imposed on South Africa, designed to bring an end to its policy of apartheid, clearly played a part in the dissolution of that country's legalized racism. However, other factors were also at play, notably widespread political activity within South Africa and strong grassroots pressure from outside that forced multinational companies to cut their ties with the country.

The sanctions imposed on South Africa were notable, in large part, because of their uniformity and cohesiveness; as many as twenty-five nations, including the United States, took part in the process at a given point. However, this was an unusual case. Frequently, sanctions are imposed by just one country, and unilateral sanctions run a much higher risk of failure.

A notable example concerns the long-standing US sanctions against Cuba. Many observers have criticized this five-decades-old economic blockade for failing to achieve its stated goal of inspiring Cubans to overthrow their country's communist leadership. Daniel Griswold, director of the Cato Institute's Center for Trade Policy Studies, argues:

> *The embargo has been a failure by every measure. It has not changed the course or nature of the Cuban government. It has not liberated a single Cuban citizen. In fact, the embargo has made the Cuban people a bit more impoverished, without making them one bit more free. At the same time, it has deprived Americans of their freedom to travel and has cost US farmers and other producers billions of dollars of potential exports.*

Several studies have indicated that the Cuban embargo is not an isolated case—that only a relatively small percentage of sanctions achieve their stated goals. Three scholars at the Institute for International Economics, Kim Elliott, Jeffrey Schott, and Gary Hufbauer, have conducted what is probably the most comprehensive study so far on United States–backed sanctions. They examined thirty-five American sanctions programs imposed between 1973 and 1996. They measured success by assessing how well the programs accomplished their stated goals, which included ending apartheid in South Africa and discouraging Libyan leader Muammar Qaddafi's support of terrorism. Using this yardstick, the scholars concluded that sanction programs worked only 23 percent of the time. Another study placed the figure somewhat higher, at about 33 percent. Even if the latter figure is accepted, however, the success rate is markedly low.

A number of observers have raised the argument that economic sanctions are not satisfactory for one specific and very important reason: the citizens of an affected nation feel the impact of sanctions long before its leaders and decision-makers do. In other words, the very groups that are the most powerless—the young, the elderly, the poor, and the sick or injured—are least able to survive the hunger, illness, and poverty that severe economic sanctions typically create.

As an example, critics point to the sanctions imposed on Iraq by the UN in the years following the Gulf War. These punitive measures did more harm than good, the critics assert: they have resulted in the deaths of thousands, aggravated an already overwhelming refugee problem, and prevented Iraq from rebuilding the necessary infrastructure to address its crises independently. Joy Gordon, a professor of philosophy at Fairfield University, comments that such severe sanctions, by denying basic humanitarian needs, are "nothing less than a deadly weapon."

Sanctions as a Symbolic Gesture

Although economic sanctions can be extremely persuasive, critics point out that they often have mixed results and can cause serious problems. One such problem may arise when sanctions are sometimes imposed even though it is acknowledged that they will be little more than symbolic—in other words, that they have only a small chance of working.

For instance, in the late 1970s, the administration of President Jimmy Carter imposed economic sanctions against the Soviet Union in a bid to induce the withdrawal of troops from Afghanistan, which the Soviets had just invaded. Carter commented at the time, "The world simply cannot stand by and

President Jimmy Carter, pictured in 1980, announces a halt in US shipments of high technology to the USSR and a partial grain-sales embargo in response to Soviet intervention in Afghanistan.

permit the Soviet Union to commit this act with impunity ... Neither the United States nor any other nation can continue to do business as usual with the Soviet Union." Carter hoped that the sanctions would appear to be a decisive move protesting the invasion. However, representatives of his administration later admitted that no one seriously believed the sanctions would be effective in ending the Soviet military incursion, and indeed they were not.

This symbolic protest was followed a few years later by actions taken by President Ronald Reagan in response to a Soviet crackdown in Poland, which was then a satellite of the USSR. These gestures were equally symbolic because they could not generate real pressure—they were imposed on a nation that did not rely on trade with the United States. This reality is reflected in the statement of an anonymous Moscow-based Western diplomat at the time: "Face it, the Soviets can buy most of the stuff they need from other countries."

Similarly, during the 1980s, sanctions by several countries against Libya's leader, Qaddafi, were not expected to end his support of terrorism primarily aimed at Israel. Rather, the sanctions were seen as an expression of serious disagreement. They were imposed mainly so that the nations in question could avoid seeming to condone Qaddafi's actions, rather than functioning as serious persuasion.

Containment Measures

Sometimes, economic sanctions and embargoes have been used in conjunction with other tactics. For example, during and after the Gulf War, the administration of President George H. W. Bush sought to impose on Iraq strict containment measures—that is, measures short of armed invasion that would still have the effect

The UN, NGOs, and the Rohingya Genocide

In August 2017, the government of Myanmar, also known as Burma, instigated widespread attacks on the Rohingya, a religious and ethnic minority in the country. As many as 725,000 people fled the violence, pouring into the country of Bangladesh, as an estimated four hundred of their villages were burned or destroyed. The international community did not step in militarily to avert this humanitarian crisis, but aid organizations flooded to their rescue.

One year later, as many as a million Rohingya were still living as refugees in the area of Cox's Bazar, a city in southern Bangladesh. The United Nations World Food Program was providing bimonthly food rations to those in the camps, the grand majority of whom could not legally work in Bangladesh and therefore could not make enough money to buy food.

NGOs also played a key role in delivering food and supplies to Rohingya refugee camps, even as seasonal flooding sometimes blocked their deliveries. Shortly after the massacres began, organizations such as Action Against Hunger, Save the Children, Doctors Without Borders, the International Rescue Committee, and BRAC, an antipoverty organization founded in Bangladesh, hurried to provide medical treatment, distribute tents, deliver water and hot food, and treat those suffering from severe trauma. The United Nations also stepped in, with such branches as the United Nations Children's Fund, or UNICEF, helping to install water pumps and provide food and supplements.

A distribution center in Bangladesh shares food with Rohingya refugees on October 10, 2017. Hundreds of people at a time line up and wait for hours to pick up packages of raw food.

In September 2018, almost one hundred agencies and NGOs were working in the camps. More than two in three were international organizations. Meanwhile, many local organizations were among the first responders to the crisis. Yet the Rohingya were living in a state of limbo, not permitted to leave the camps and enter Bangladeshi society and unable to return home, and the ability of aid organizations to provide long-term aid was being put to the test. The UN Refugee Agency issued calls for more financial help from the international community in mid-2018 as the wait continued. Without the aid of the UN and NGOs, it is doubtless that this humanitarian crisis of devastating proportions would have been much, much worse.

of curtailing Saddam Hussein's aggression. This was, however, only a partial success. Political analyst Michael Walzer explains:

> *The harsh containment system imposed on Iraq after the first Gulf War was an experiment in responding differently. Containment had three elements:*
>
> *The first was an embargo intended to prevent the importation of arms, which also affected supplies of food and medicine—it should have been possible to design a smarter set of sanctions.*
>
> *The second element was an inspection system, organized by the UN, to block the domestic development of weapons of mass destruction.*
>
> *The third element was the establishment of no-fly zones in the northern and southern parts of the country so that Iraq's air power could not be used against its own people.*

The system, Walzer concludes, was effective in preventing mass murder and the development of weapons, but it failed to prevent the Iraq War, which began in 2003.

Long-standing restrictions imposed on Iran represent another example of US economic sanctions. These penalties were imposed because of evidence that the Iranian government has supported anti-American terrorism. Still another example is a joint sanction with the European Union against Myanmar (Burma) because of its record of human rights violations and political repression.

Nongovernmental Agencies

In addition to sanctions and other forms of nonmilitary intervention, the work of nongovernmental organizations (NGOs) must also be taken into account. As the name implies,

NGOs are groups independent of national governments or the UN. Among the most prominent of these are Médicins Sans Frontières (Doctors Without Borders), the Red Cross, and Amnesty International.

Groups like these provide what some analysts call "politics short of force." In addition to performing vital work such as emergency medical and famine response, they also create far-reaching information sources that can bring violations of human rights or acts of repression to the world's attention. In this way, NGOs seek to stabilize a volatile or dangerous situation, then aid in the formation of a civil, peaceful society.

In time, it is hoped, this stability will result in forums for free speech, the formation of political parties and watchdog agencies for rights abuses, and other hallmarks of a free society. Some analysts stress that NGOs are most effective when they operate in conjunction with more formal, government-sponsored measures such as economic sanctions. Walzer writes: "These organizations, and these men and women, are at least potential contributors to a democratic political process ... In fact, we have to sponsor and support this interaction—because these two together can help us avoid war itself."

However, in their day-to-day operations, NGOs take on the foremost task of responding to humanitarian crises quickly, in much the same way that governments might and sometimes do. Again and again, they have succeeded in curbing the worst possible outcomes of conflict, war, genocide, famine, and crimes against humanity.

Chapter Four

ARGUMENTS IN FAVOR

Not all military interventions have been legally or ethically justifiable. Some were motivated by greed or a desire for power on the part of national leaders. Others were executed poorly or proved ineffective. However, when it comes time to weigh a nation's right to self-determination and practical concerns against humanitarian, economic, or political drivers, there are no easy decisions. What's more, some interventions have proven instrumental in preventing the loss of human life or averting crisis.

Such situations raise hard questions. Are most nonviolent responses to aggression doomed to failure? Is a pacifist world possible? Leaders may be fully and passionately committed to governing through

Opposite: During D-Day in 1944, Allied forces land at Omaha Beach in Normandy, France. Many Allies joined World War II to aid countries such as France that had been invaded by Nazi Germany.

nonviolence, but are there times when this is not enough? And, if a military strike is needed, how should it be carried out?

Countless ideas and theories have emerged in an effort to answer these and other thorny questions. Broadly speaking, many of these ideas can be brought together in what is known as the theory of just war. This theory is an effort to define under what circumstances armed aggression could be acceptable.

Supporters of just-war theory argue that at times there is really no choice at all. The consequences of inaction would be so severe, they say, that not using force would be morally wrong. The classic example cited is World War II.

Just-war advocates point out that the nonmilitary responses to Nazi aggression in the 1930s failed to prevent full-blown war. It soon became abundantly clear that armed resistance was the only option if Hitler's war machine was to be stopped. Since the Nazis and the other Axis powers, Italy and Japan, posed a clear and immediate threat to the survival of other nations, the war against the Axis powers was generally seen as fully justified—and it was perhaps as "popular" as a war can be. There was opposition in some quarters, certainly, but these voices over time became the minority.

A Legally Justifiable Option

Sometimes a natural disaster or famine produces chaos, looting, and other situations with the potential for escalating violence that leave the affected populations defenseless. If a country cannot handle the crisis on its own, there is relatively little ambiguity: armed intervention is likely the right response.

However, real-world situations are rarely that simple. The moral argument, defining the response as "simply the right thing to do," cannot be the only factor in deciding whether a given intervention fits the criteria for a just war. The legal ramifications must also be taken into account, such as a possible breach of the

Geneva Conventions concerning the humanitarian treatment of victims of war.

This legal aspect is, however, a notoriously difficult concept to pin down. One nation may consider an intervention legally and morally justifiable—but another nation, whether directly involved or not, may have different interpretations of the law, the facts, or both.

For example, in what ways might Iran view the presence of US naval forces in the Persian Gulf? As a sign of imminent attack, or as a force meant to safeguard humanitarian concerns in the region? Or, to take another example: all nations experience crime within their borders. But when do "everyday" crimes, such as murder or aggravated assault, escalate into genocide—at which point another country might intervene? What about human rights violations that do not necessarily result in death or injury, such as the repression of free speech or the forced evacuation of a population? At what point do these improper acts justify armed intervention from a legal perspective?

To be effective in such situations, and to make a solid case for intervening, laws must achieve a delicate balance. If they are too broad, they include so much ambiguity that they are essentially meaningless. The result can be serious abuses of power disguised as benevolent actions. If laws are too narrow, however, they may not cover all potential situations and so run the risk of being ineffective.

Of course, there are other factors to consider when a government is making a legal case for armed intervention. One important question concerns the aftermath. Will there be sufficient follow-through? Accepting the responsibility of intervening means committing to dealing with the consequences. In other words, it is not enough to solve an immediate crisis and leave. The intervening nation has both a legal and moral responsibility to provide the groundwork for long-lasting stability. As Walzer explains, "[A] foreign state or coalition of states that sends an army across the border to stop the killing is also going to have to replace the government or, at least, to begin the process of replacement."

In short, it is difficult—perhaps impossible—to find a "one-size-fits-all" remedy that is also enforceable. Nonetheless, in an effort to answer such questions, just-war theory has been woven into several documents generally respected as having the force of law, notably the United Nations Charter and the Geneva Conventions. The Geneva Conventions outline legally acceptable and humanitarian treatment of prisoners of war. Just-war theory, as a result, has become a cornerstone of international law.

Protecting National Security

Timing is yet another major factor to be considered in building a case for armed response to perceived aggression. Governments often rely on a concept called preemptive or anticipatory self-defense. This idea focuses on nullifying threats before they reach a nation's borders—in other words, striking before being struck.

It is crucial here to distinguish between preemption and prevention. An example of a preemptive act would be a nation striking a foreign army that is clearly preparing to violate the first nation's border country; preemption is considered to be legal under international law. Prevention, on the other hand, is an attack that is launched before a particular threat to national security has materialized—for example, the US invasions in the two Gulf Wars.

The distinction is not always easy to make. Military and political scholars have been trying for hundreds of years to express, clearly and unambiguously, the legal differences between preemption and prevention. Recent shifts in the conduct of global affairs, notably the rise of international terrorism, have further complicated the question. Christopher Preble, vice president for defense and foreign policy studies at the Cato Institute, points out the ambiguities that arise with respect to threats posed by groups, such as terrorist organizations, that are not tied to single, distinct nations: "[I]n a world where nonstate actors appear to pose a greater threat to peace and security than do states, do the rules designed to constrain states need to be revisited? Is there too little war in the world, or too much? Do states resort to war too frequently, or not often enough?"

Anticipatory action is not new, of course, but it has grown significantly more common in recent decades. Advocates of such proactive intervention point out that time is of the essence when a nation perceives a threat. Simply put, the nation cannot afford to wait; moving too slowly would render its self-defense forces useless.

This raises difficult questions. At what point is there strong enough reason to believe that an attack is imminent? If it is indeed imminent, must any legal measures of anticipatory action be followed in order to justify it to the rest of the world?

The argument against anticipatory intervention is that it is unacceptable to punish a nation for an offense that it has not yet committed. However, this position can be countered by asserting that it is too dangerous for a nation or multilateral force to wait for overt aggression. According to Walzer, a number of factors favor the legitimacy of a preemptive strike. These include the seriousness of the anticipated aggression; the kind and quality of evidence required to evaluate the situation; the speed with which leaders must decide; the issue of fairness; and the duty to protect citizens.

Preemptive strikes for any reason, including national security, are currently forbidden according to the UN Charter unless authorized in advance by the Security Council. Nonetheless, some countries have, at times, asserted the right to strike first. A prominent example of this was the 2003 US-led strike on Iraq that launched the Iraq War.

In December 2003, still early in the Iraq War, US soldiers search a house in Tikrit, Iraq, as an Iraqi woman and her children wait outside.

The 2003 invasion was not authorized by the UN, received little global support, and was condemned by many countries. Then UN secretary-general Kofi Annan was also critical, telling reporters, "I hope we do not see another Iraq-type operation for a long time—without UN approval and [without] much broader support from the international community ... [F]rom the charter point of view, it was illegal."

Related to this is the question of backlash justification. Belarus and other nations have on occasion used US actions—such as the rapid increase in security measures within its own borders taken by the Department of Homeland Security—as justification for relaxing their controls against human rights abuses, such as violations of the rights of Belarus's ethnic Polish population. They argue that the United States is curtailing the rights of its own citizens, so other countries are justified in curtailing rights within their own borders for the sake of fighting terrorism. Thomas Carothers, a scholar at the Carnegie Endowment for International Peace, comments:

Ironically, and also sadly, ... the greatest source of negative ripple effects has come from the [George W. Bush] administration's pursuit of the war on terrorism at home. The heightened terrorist threat has inevitably put pressure on US civil liberties. But the administration failed to strike the right balance early on, unnecessarily abridging or abusing rights through the large-scale detention of immigrants, closed deportation hearings, and the declaration of some US citizens as "enemy combatants" with no right to counsel or even to contest the designation.

Shifting Presidential Policies

Despite such criticism, the administration of George W. Bush adamantly asserted the right to launch a preemptive invasion of Iraq on the grounds of Iraq's alleged buildup of weapons of mass destruction. The administration's position was detailed in what has become known as the Bush Doctrine.

This policy held that the United States has the right to intervene militarily in countries that harbor or aid terrorist groups, since those groups pose a clear threat to national security. In a document called "The National Security Strategy of the United States," administration officials wrote:

[T]he first duty of the United States Government remains what it always has been: to protect the American people and American interests. It is an enduring American principle that this duty obligates the government to anticipate and counter threats, using all elements of national power, before the threats can do grave damage. The greater the threat, the greater

Ways to Prevent Armed Conflict

Kofi Annan, secretary-general of the United Nations from 1997 to 2006, was one of the world's most eloquent advocates of preventing armed conflict through peaceful means. In 1999, he summarized some of the primary causes of armed intervention, and some ways to prevent it:

> For early prevention to be effective, the multidimensional root causes of conflict need to be identified and addressed. The proximate [immediate] cause of conflict may be an outbreak of public disorder or a protest over a particular incident, but the root cause may be, for example, socio-economic inequities and inequalities, systematic ethnic discrimination, denial of human rights, disputes over political participation or long-standing grievances over land and other resource allocation.

The reaction from society and political leaders may be dramatically different in each nation, Annan explained. For instance, if that country's institutions respect the rule of law—the application of the law equally to all groups of people—then it may be more likely to weather and manage internal conflicts independent of the need for outside help.

A more nuanced understanding of the factors contributing to any given conflict is essential for the international community as it decides how to react to a conflict in a particular nation, Annan added. It can help determine whether armed intervention is, in fact, the most effective solution. "The need for reliable early-warning information and a deep and careful understanding of local circumstances and traditions is therefore of great importance, and the fundamental inequities need to be identified and addressed in development planning and programming," Annan asserted.

is the risk of inaction—and the more compelling the case for taking anticipatory action to defend ourselves, even if uncertainty remains as to the time and place of the enemy's attack.

Bush's successor, Barack Obama, expressed his personal distaste for overly rigid guidelines in international affairs. Obama and Secretary of State Hillary Clinton stressed reliance on negotiation and collaboration, when possible, but decided to intervene in Libya in 2011, when they felt it was not possible.

Actions taken during the first years of the Obama administration seemed to imply that Obama had taken a less aggressive approach than that outlined in the Bush Doctrine. Obama expounded on the need for the United States to disentangle itself from the conflicts in Iraq and Afghanistan. Stepping away from conflicts to which the United States had already committed, however, proved

After 9/11, President George W. Bush demanded that Afghanistan turn over Osama bin Laden.

difficult. In February 2010, journalist William Pfaff explained: "In Afghanistan and Iraq, the U.S. found itself mired in interventions it has been unable successfully to conclude. It has [also] found itself drawn into deeper and much more dangerous engagements in the political and military affairs of Pakistan, the Iran nuclear imbroglio and an out-of-control Israeli government."

Obama is not the first president to have inherited a complex situation. He had to cope with the consequences of interventionist tactics and strategies that began long before his term of office. As former secretary of state Madeleine Albright remarked, "Presidents do not inherit a clean slate."

However, by 2013, Peter Feaver, writing for *Foreign Policy*, concluded that Obama had in fact embraced "at least the preemption part of the Bush doctrine" to justify his administration's use of drone strikes in Pakistan and the Middle East as part of counterterrorism efforts. The administration had adopted the policy that an adversary need only pose an "imminent" threat against the United States to justify such strikes. What's more, according to a memo, the country's legal right to make preemptive strikes "does not require the United States to have clear evidence that a specific attack on U.S. persons and interests will take place in the immediate future." During his time in office, President Obama authorized 542 drone strikes, which killed approximately 3,797 people, including more than 300 civilians, according to Micah Zenko, writing for the Council on Foreign Relations, a nonpartisan think tank.

Others, however, have pointed to the Joint Comprehensive Plan of Action (JCPOA) as evidence of Obama's rejection of the Bush Doctrine. The JCPOA was an agreement with Iran to lift sanctions in exchange for limiting its nuclear program. The multilateral action was reached after years of diplomatic talks. President Donald Trump would later withdraw from the deal, constituting a return in many ways to the Bush Doctrine, argues conservative opinion magazine the *Weekly Standard*.

When it comes to the Trump administration, some have argued that President Trump doesn't have a clear and defined approach to foreign policy. Then White House press secretary Sean Spicer outlined what he called the "Trump Doctrine" as an America-first policy in April 2017: "We're not just going to

A scientific compound in Syria was destroyed by US airstrikes in 2018 in response to an alleged chemical-weapons attack by Syria.

become the world's policeman running around the world, but [the Trump Doctrine is] that we have to have a clear and defined national interest wherever we act, and that it's our national security, first and foremost, that has to deal with how we act."

Some have insisted, though, that Trump's intervention in Syria did not respond to a national-security threat and therefore did not align with the Trump Doctrine as Spicer described it. In April 2018, the United States retaliated with airstrikes against key sites in Syria after Syrian president Bashar al-Assad reportedly used chemical weapons against his own people. The United Kingdom and France joined the United States in the strikes, although there was some controversy about who had been responsible for the chemical attacks and whether other nations had the right to step in. Trump had launched similar strikes in retaliation for chemical weapons use a year before.

Spicer, however, argued that the use of chemical weapons does constitute a "clear danger to our country and to our people."

Spreading Ideologies

One reason often advanced to justify armed intervention has been used for thousands of years: the desire to spread a particular ideology. History shows that force has frequently been used to impose religious beliefs (such as Christianity or Islam) or political philosophies (such as communism or democracy) on other peoples or nations. The United States has intervened for ideological reasons on a number of occasions. For instance, when President Lyndon Johnson authorized the use of troops in the Dominican Republic in 1965 to forestall what he called "a second Cuba," Johnson stated:

> *Over the years of our history our forces have gone forth into many lands, but always they returned when they were no longer needed. For the purpose of America is never to suppress liberty, but always to save it. The purpose of America is never to take freedom, but always to return it; never to break pace but to bolster it, and never to seize land but always to save lives.*

A related argument in the case for armed intervention concerns struggles for independence. Efforts by breakaway regions to become separate nations have often resulted in invasions by "parent" nations. Recent examples include separatist movements in East Timor (from Indonesia), Tibet (from China), and Chechnya (from Russia).

In the wake of the September 11 attacks, the US position changed dramatically in favor of supporting the struggles of populations wishing to break away from an oppressive parent. The George W. Bush administration saw this support as key to combating anti-American terrorism. It therefore launched initiatives to foster emerging democratic movements on several continents. A statement issued by the Defense Department in 2008 stressed that the government's policy was vital to "promoting freedom, justice and human dignity by working to end tyranny, promote effective democracies and extend prosperity; and confronting the challenges of our time by leading a growing community of democracies."

At first, the Obama administration downplayed the use of military intervention in the spread of democracy. This modification reflected Obama's emphasis on increased diplomatic efforts, rather than proactive military measures, to resolve international disputes. However, President Obama also acknowledged the need to remain open to the possibility that armed intervention may be necessary in some cases. In his remarks before the Nobel Prize committee in 2009, he stated:

> *The world rallied around America after the 9/11 attacks, and continues to support our efforts in Afghanistan, because of the horror of those senseless attacks and the recognized principle of self-defense. Likewise, the world recognized the need to confront Saddam Hussein when he invaded Kuwait—a consensus that sent a clear message to all about the cost of aggression.*

Achieving this kind of international consensus and respecting the law is essential if intervention is to be justified, Obama added: "America [cannot insist]—in fact, no nation—can insist that others follow the rules of the road if we refuse to follow them ourselves.

For when we don't, our actions appear arbitrary and undercut the legitimacy of future interventions, no matter how justified."

In the spring of 2011, the Obama administration teamed up with NATO nations to intervene in a conflict in Libya. Some people felt Obama contradicted himself by intervening without consulting Congress.

Standing up for Human Rights

The close and sometimes ambiguous connection between the need for humanitarian aid and the use of armed intervention has been the source of many dilemmas in the recent past. In the years after World War II, a number of theorists and diplomats set out to formally clarify fundamental principles and policies of humanitarian aid. These principles naturally included ideas about the legitimate application of armed intervention. Since then, the issue of humanitarian aid has become a vitally important part of the process when making a case for armed intervention.

Kofi Annan, who was the UN's secretary-general between 1997 and 2006, was a major driving force behind this push to clarify the legitimate use of force in the name of humanitarian aid. Early in his tenure at the helm of the UN, Annan challenged the world's leaders by asking, "If humanitarian intervention is, indeed, an unacceptable assault on sovereignty, how should we respond to … gross and systematic violations of human rights that affect every precept of our common humanity?"

In 2001, the International Commission on Intervention and State Sovereignty formally articulated a concept called "responsibility to protect," or R2P. The report of this special agency, which was sponsored by the Canadian government, was followed in 2004 by another report from the secretary-general's High-Level Panel on Threats, Challenges and Change. It asserted that diplomacy should be stressed and armed intervention used

Kofi Annan, a former secretary-general of the United Nations, sought to identify when force is necessary for humanitarian reasons.

only as a last resort. The report further stated that governments have the primary responsibility to protect their own citizens from catastrophes; however, when a given government is unable or unwilling to act appropriately, "that responsibility should be taken up by the wider international community, with it spanning a continuum involving prevention, response to violence, if necessary, and rebuilding shattered societies."

Acting on these reports, diplomats at the UN drafted Resolution 1674, which the organization formally adopted in 2006. The document articulates the UN Security Council's position that the nations of the world have a responsibility, not merely an option, to protect the civilian populations of other countries in the name of just humanitarian causes.

Citing genocide, war crimes, ethnic cleansing, and crimes against humanity, the resolution specifically asserts that nations give up the right to resolve extraordinary internal affairs if it has been determined that they cannot or will not do so on their own. The resolution states that R2P's core tenet "is that sovereignty entails responsibility. Each state has a responsibility to protect its citizens; if a state is unable or unwilling to carry out that function, the state abrogates [gives up] its sovereignty, at which point both the right and the responsibility to remedy the situation falls on the international community."

However, the Security Council stopped short of providing authorization for intervention beyond this general statement. It was not able to find enough common ground among nations to create enforceable new international conventions or to amend its own charter. Regarding the use of force, the body's statement was vague, asserting only that armed intervention was a last resort but leaving open the question of how it should be applied.

The practical value of the resolution has therefore been passionately criticized and debated. Some experts argue that R2P is toothless. Others call the action taken so far by the UN a significant step forward. In either case, Annan's successor, Ban Ki-Moon, remained a firm advocate of R2P. In 2009, he wrote that the secretary-general "must be the spokesperson for the vulnerable and the threatened when their Governments become their persecutors instead of their protectors or can no longer shield them from marauding armed groups."

Meanwhile, the US military and government have developed a separate set of policies concerning armed intervention for humanitarian purposes. These policies go beyond what the UN resolution requires of member nations. Specifically, they authorize the use of force (up to and including deadly force) to combat widespread, systematic violence against the innocent, including murder, physical assault, torture, and sexual assault. The criteria for initiating force are given in what are called the Rules of Engagement (ROE). However, the ROE stipulate that any such force must be kept to a minimum.

Defending National Territory

The right to defend one's lawful territory is, of course, closely intertwined with any argument for or against intervention. This question concerns what theorists call the concept of sovereignty, or the idea that nations have an absolute right to defend their physical territory against invasion. Acceptance of the concept has been a fundamental part of international relations for thousands of years. The UN Charter makes explicit its respect for this basic tenet of politics, prohibiting nations from using or threatening to use force to encroach on the territorial integrity of others:

> *[N]othing contained in the present Charter shall authorize the United Nations to intervene in matters which are essentially within the domestic jurisdiction*

Some forty thousand Albanian refugees from the conflict in Kosovo occupy a camp in Macedonia in 1999.

of any state or shall require the Members to submit such matters to settlement under the present Charter, but this principle shall not prejudice the application of enforcement measures under Chapter VII [of the Charter].

However, in recent decades, the traditional standard of sovereignty has begun to shift. Among some academics, military leaders, politicians, and other experts, a theory called "contingent sovereignty" is gaining favor. Simply put, proponents of contingent sovereignty argue that a nation does not have an absolute and total right to defend its physical borders. They assert instead that the use of military intervention that violates borders is legitimate if people behind a given border are in danger.

Contingent sovereignty began to gain favor in the wake of widespread atrocities of the mid- and late twentieth century, as represented by the horrors of the Holocaust, the cruelties of the Stalin-era Soviet Union, the killing fields of Cambodia, and ethnic massacres in Rwanda and elsewhere. According to this theory, a nation gives up its sovereign rights if it oppresses or makes war on segments of its own population. The same is true if it tacitly allows atrocities—that is, if it cannot or will not prevent a segment of its population from oppressing another. In such a case, other nations have an obligation to restore order and peace.

Contingent sovereignty in action can be seen in the bloody dispute between Serbs and ethnic Albanians in the former Yugoslavia, which is now referred to as the Kosovo crisis. Yugoslavia's leader, Slobodan Milosevic, was a Serb, and he allowed widespread political repression, catastrophic economic depression, and crippling unemployment to oppress his country's citizens, who were ethnic Albanians. When this population broke away and declared the independent Republic of Kosovo in 1999, Serbian forces retaliated with massive and violent ethnic cleansing that involved rapes, deaths, and forced displacement. The international community intervened militarily to stop the violence.

The nations of NATO used the concept of contingent sovereignty as justification to intervene militarily in Kosovo on the grounds that Milosevic had given up his sovereign rights by refusing to control the Serbian population. NATO also pointed out that the conflict posed a direct threat to its members' own security.

The intervention occurred, however, without the support of the UN Security Council, which failed to approve any resolution authorizing force. Despite this, NATO persevered, since it saw its mission as an attempt to address a humanitarian crisis in a timely way—a goal that had not been achieved in 1994 in the African nation of Rwanda, where the international community badly botched an opportunity to bring a halt to genocide.

It was not absolutely necessary that the United States and its NATO allies intervene in Kosovo, since Milosevic was not supporting terrorist operations against them; nor did the region have valuable resources to protect. There was little self-interest involved. However, the United States and its allies hoped that intervention would help create an important precedent for the future. They wanted to avoid another Rwanda. As political science experts Derek Chollet and James Goldgeier put it, "[T]his time they would seize the opportunity to right a new wrong."

Achieving Widespread Security

Another justification offered up for armed intervention is the pursuit of collective security. This concept refers to alliances among countries to guarantee that any one nation will not need to act on its own, with no backing from others. The United Nations, NATO, the African Union, and the Non-Aligned Movement, an organization of nations not affiliated with any great power, are four organizations devoted to collective security. Such alliances, of course, can work both ways—that is, they can both initiate and resist armed intervention in cases where individual countries might fail.

Advocates of such multilateral alliances argue that they are not just expedient but also necessary to achieve legitimacy for armed intervention. It is also essential, they stress, that nations share the burden equitably. As Walzer explains, "If measures ... are to work against evil or dangerous regimes, they have to be the common work of a group of nations ... Collective security must be a collective project. It won't be successful if the costs of security are assigned to one state while all the others pursue business as usual."

Although many insist that there are, in some cases, good reasons for engaging in a military intervention, very few would argue that armed intervention is always the most effective policy for resolving conflict in another nation. That is why, to this day, international organizations, politicians, nations, experts, and analysts are still seeking to define a clear set of guidelines for when armed intervention is justified, legal, and unavoidable.

Chapter Five

ARGUMENTS IN OPPOSITION

In most cases where military intervention is deemed necessary, intervening nations have first explored the possibility of a diplomatic or nonviolent resolution to the conflict at hand. Organizations such as the United Nations exist for the explicit purpose of seeking nonmilitary solutions by facilitating international cooperation and diplomacy. Because of resources such as these—or, alternatively, because of a strong belief in and respect for national sovereignty—some might even argue that there is rarely or never a situation in which armed intervention is justifiable.

Opposite: In a rally in New York City on April 29, 2006, veterans of the Iraq War speak out against that very war and the policies of US president George W. Bush.

The Pacifist Perspective

A pacifist would say it's never right to use military force. Broadly speaking, pacifists reject violence as the means to an end. They argue that violence, or even the threat of violence, is almost never, if ever, justified. Strict pacifism holds that war is always wrong and that there is always a better resolution to the problem than fighting. Less-strict pacifists may concede that violence might be justified in extreme circumstances where there is an immediate danger.

Many pacifist organizations are devoted to campaigns of nonviolent civil disobedience, perhaps combined with international diplomatic and economic sanctions. Such nonviolent protest, they contend, can be as effective as war in expelling an aggressor nation, with far less destruction of lives or property. In offering examples of widespread political change brought about largely through nonviolence, pacifists point to Mahatma Gandhi's independence movement in India and to the end of apartheid in South Africa. Ethics professor Brian Orend outlines the steps by which a determined pacifist resistance might bring about the downfall of a repressive regime:

> *After all, the pacifist might say, no invader could possibly maintain its grip on the conquered nation in light of such systematic isolation, non-cooperation and non-violent resistance. How could it work the factories, harvest the fields, or run the stores, when everyone would be striking? How could it maintain the will to keep the country in the face of crippling economic sanctions and diplomatic censure from the international community?*

A Question of Proportionality

In addition to the matter of necessity, another factor to consider is what may be called proportionality. Simply put, do the ends justify the means? Assuming that the intended outcome is achieved, will it be worth the resulting damage to (or sacrifices by) the aggressor nation? Will this be true for the aggressor's allies as well?

Charles Hauss is a senior fellow for innovation at the Alliance for Peacebuilding, a network of more than one hundred organizations working toward finding nonviolent ways to manage conflict. Hauss has identified four basic questions that the leaders of nations must ask when considering the worthiness of an intervention.

First of all, Hauss asks, "Why does military intervention occur in some cases but not others?" The answer may include one or more reasons, notably humanitarian concerns or issues of national security.

Second, "What determines whether an intervention will succeed or fail?" Though success can be difficult to measure or quantify, Hauss points out that interventions generally have at least one goal in mind against which their results can be measured.

The third question on Hauss's list is whether a given intervention will ultimately lead to peace and stability. This question is especially thorny if the intervention would involve incursions to support the weaker side of an uneven conflict.

Finally, Hauss adds, leaders must ask "about the relationship between states whose military forces intervene and the NGOs who have long provided relief and other aid to civilians caught up in the fighting. [Many NGOs] have abandoned their traditional and ... vital political neutrality in order to get the funds and the influence that cooperation with states provide[s], thereby diluting their own long-term impact."

Proportionality also raises the question of backlash. If the intervention is to relieve suffering by allowing humanitarian aid, might the action anger the offending government enough to create still more misery and destruction? What about reactions from other countries and groups around the world—would widespread negative opinion have a significant effect? The same question applies to public opinion within the intervening nation: would a controversial intervention create instability and widespread protests, as was the case in the United States during the Vietnam War?

In short, will the cure be worse than the disease? It is, of course, impossible to predict the future, but it is possible to make decisions based on likely outcomes. As Orend writes:

> *A state must, prior to initiating [armed intervention or war], weigh the universal goods expected to result from it … against the universal evils expected to result, notably casualties. Only if the benefits are proportional to, or "worth" the costs, may the war action proceed. (The universal must be stressed, since often in war states only tally their own expected benefits and costs, radically discounting those accruing to the enemy and to any innocent third parties.)*

Chance of Success

Along with necessity and proportionality, a third important consideration in any argument about military intervention concerns the chance that it will achieve its goals in both the short and the long term. The failure of an intervention will obviously result in failure to stop the immediate problem. Moreover, even if the intervention is successful, violence may simply resume after the intervening troops have withdrawn.

This reflects back to the concept of proportionality. Could a reasonable person predict that the outcome of an intervention would be worse than the result of doing nothing at all? Proponents of one common argument against the use of military intervention refer to the backlog of historic examples of outright failures, such as the Soviet venture in Afghanistan, and disastrous "incompletes" like the US intervention in Iraq.

The situation in Kosovo offers another example. Even before US involvement, it appeared that Kosovo had the potential to become unmanageable. However, General Colin Powell, then the chairman of the US Joint Chiefs of Staff, felt that intervening in the conflict would be a misstep for the United States. Speaking about involvement in the Balkans, he warned, "No American President could defend to the American people the heavy sacrifice of lives it would cost to resolve this baffling conflict."

Kosovo did indeed turn out to be a difficult problem for the United States. Even though NATO's armed intervention there came to an end in 1999, the situation has yet to be satisfactorily resolved for America. In large part, this has been because the interests of three important parties remain in conflict: when Kosovo declared independence in 2008, the United States supported its right to autonomous self-governance, and Serbia and Russia did not. As this debate has gone on, meanwhile, NATO has continued to monitor the situation in an effort to maintain peace. The International Court of Justice ruled its declaration legal in 2010, though Serbia still does not support it.

Failure in Somalia

Another example of a failed intervention that was far more damaging than it should have been occurred in the early 1990s in Somalia, a nation in northeast Africa. Brigadier General John S. Brown, former chief of military history for the US Army, summarizes:

US Marines guard a C-141 Starlifter transport plane in December 1992 as citizens of Somalia crowd around.

The United States Army has a long tradition of humanitarian relief. No such operation has proven as costly or shocking, however, as that undertaken in Somalia from August 1992 to March 1994. Greeted initially by Somalis happy to be saved from starvation, U.S. troops were slowly drawn into interclan power struggles and ill-defined "nation-building" missions.

In Somalia, decades of fighting among rival clan warlords had resulted in widespread ethnic cleansing, homelessness, famine, and poverty. Estimates of casualties vary widely, but the number of casualties in the Somali civil war almost certainly reached several hundred thousand.

Hoping to stabilize the situation, the United States, the UN, and the African Union sent peacekeeping troops to Somalia. The purpose was not to take sides in the fighting but to facilitate the delivery of aid to areas that needed it the most. At its peak, late in 1992, twenty-six thousand American troops were stationed in the region, although this was quickly reduced to about five thousand by May 1993, when the worst of the crisis seemed to be over.

Immediately after this partial withdrawal, the bulk of the peacekeeping was turned over to a multinational force under UN control. However, these troops were unable to maintain order. The UN troops, and the remaining US forces, suffered significant casualties as the violence continued, most of them in the intense Battle of Mogadishu in October 1993. In addition, more UN troops and many civilians were also wounded or killed. In a further humiliation, crowds of local civilians and Somali National Alliance soldiers (who served Somali warlord Mohamed Farrah Aidid) dragged the bodies of American soldiers through the streets of Mogadishu, the capital city. This episode later became the subject of the book and film *Black Hawk Down*. (The title refers to the two Black Hawk helicopters shot down during the fight.)

Lessons Learned in Somalia

In the wake of the disastrous Battle of Mogadishu, the Clinton administration determined that success in Somalia would not be possible without a full-scale military operation, and this was deemed to be ill-advised. US troops were then withdrawn from the region. The conflict among rival clans continues today, and Somalia remains a volatile country.

The failed operation in Somalia has significantly affected subsequent debate over the advisability of armed intervention in Africa and elsewhere, even for a clearly defined case of humanitarian aid. In an article entitled "Somalia and the Future of Humanitarian Intervention" in the magazine *Foreign Affairs*, foreign policy experts Walter Clarke and Jeffrey Herbst take note of this. They cite as direct results of the disastrous experience in

Refugees of the violent genocide in Rwanda in 1994 flee the capital city of Kigali, carrying their belongings.

Somalia the failure of the world to intervene effectively in later civil wars. In the horrifying clash between rival Hutu and Tutsi clans in the central African nation of Rwanda, for example, death estimates vary between five hundred thousand and one million. The ethnic cleansing in Bosnia was equally horrifying. Clarke and Herbst write:

> [The] refusal to respond to the genocide in Rwanda that began in April 1994 was due in part to [the military] retreat from Somalia, announced after the deaths of 18 U.S. Army Rangers on October 3–4, 1993. In Bosnia, UN peacekeepers under fire from or taken prisoner by Serb forces ... were expected to turn the other cheek for fear of "crossing the Mogadishu line."

A Policy of Nonintervention

The policy known as nonintervention is an essential mainstay in any argument against armed intervention. As the name implies, nonintervention holds that a nation has restricted rights to aggressively enter the territory of another country; moreover, each nation is considered to be responsible for addressing its own problems only. The primary goal, of course, is to avoid expensive, bloody, uncertain, and unpopular conflict.

The Case for Noninterventionism

A 2016 poll conducted by the Pew Research Center found that 57 percent of Americans believe that the United States should let other nations handle their own problems "as best they can," compared to just 37 percent who thought the United States should "help other countries deal with their problems." A majority of Americans, it seems, seem to oppose intervention—or, at least, excessive intervention.

Congressman Ron Paul of Texas was one of the most prominent US politicians espousing a policy of noninterventionism in foreign affairs in recent years. In his view, the actions of the US government should be consistent with those of the Founding Fathers, who generally favored noninterventionist ideas.

During a debate in 2007, Paul addressed President W. Bush's statement in his second Inaugural Address that "[i]t is the policy of the US to seek and support the growth of democratic movements and institutions in every nation and culture."

Paul responded: "Our responsibility is to spread democracy here, make sure that we have it. This is a philosophic and foreign policy problem, because what the president was saying was just a continuation of Woodrow Wilson's 'making the world safe for democracy.' There's nothing wrong with spreading our values around the world, but it is wrong to spread it by force. We should spread it by setting an example and going and doing a good job here."

Nonintervention does not, however, mean that a nation must cut itself off entirely from the rest of the world. In theory, at least, a country's noninterventionist policy applies only to armed intervention. It can still maintain full economic and diplomatic ties with other nations. Furthermore, noninterventionists often make allowances for a temporary relaxation of this "hands-off" policy. For example, they may suspend their principles in the face of aggression that is a direct threat to the nation's self-preservation.

US supporters of nonintervention believe that the nation's overall foreign policy has as its primary goal the fostering of peace, freedom, and democracy around the world. However, they assert, this goal can be achieved without resorting to military intervention. Their position is that cultural exchanges, trade and economic aid programs, technical or social assistance, and other forms of support are more effective.

Isolationism

The related policy of isolationism is essentially a more extreme version of nonintervention. This is a far more conservative policy, advocating restricted trade and diplomatic relations—sometimes toward friends and foes alike. Isolationism instead stresses economic protectionism, strong restrictions on immigration, and other policies designed to make a nation as self-sufficient as possible. This approach holds that the desire to rectify another country's internal problems does not necessarily create the authority or justification for aggressive action, even in the name of humanitarian aid.

One vocal spokesman for severely limiting or even eliminating intervention for humanitarian purposes is policy expert, human rights advocate, and author David Rieff. In a speech before the Carnegie Council, a distinguished organization devoted to supporting ethical leadership in global politics, Rieff explained why he strongly supports human rights but does not believe that

Author David Rieff, who opposes most interventions for humanitarian purposes, speaks at a 2006 event in New York City.

armed intervention is the answer to abuses. He pointed out that the people most affected by intervention are too often those who have no say in drafting human rights regulations. In Rieff's opinion, much of the world regards the UN as consistently backing up self-interested US policies in the name of human rights:

> [I]n the rest of the world—[and this is] something that people in Washington find hard to credit—this commitment to human rights looks an awful lot like American imperialism, and the UN ... looks rather like the constabulary that cleans up after the Americans, after all is finished ... [T]he problem is that what seems like straightforward intervening on the part of the interveners here looks astonishingly like recolonization there.

A Brief History of Isolationism

In the opinions of many experts, isolationism is not always a practical option. World economic factors are generally considered to be an important part of this argument. Historically, nations both large and small have always been dependent, at least to a degree, on foreign trade, and so must maintain a spirit of cooperation. In the eyes of analysts who reject the isolationist position, self-sufficiency, however admirable it might be, is not a truly realistic goal.

However, over the course of history, isolationism has often been an important part of foreign policy debate. Since American independence, degrees of isolationism and nonintervention have been major factors in ongoing US considerations of national policy and, by extension, in the question of armed intervention as well. George Washington and Thomas Jefferson were only two of the policy's strongest supporters during the nation's early years. Furthermore, until fairly recently, isolationism has been a key factor in every major war in which the United States has been involved.

For example, the country initially avoided armed participation in World War I, restricting itself to supplying military aid to European allies. When German submarines began directly attacking US ships, however, American leaders were prompted to authorize the use of arms. This move, which had widespread public support, ended what had been broad national approval of a policy of nonintervention. When the war was over, however, public support of an isolationist posture returned to favor. This popular mindset had also been a major factor in the United States' failure to join the League of Nations.

Isolationist or noninterventionist tendencies, largely suppressed during World War II, remained weak among American leaders in the middle of the twentieth century, as fears of communism took hold. During the Cold War, the United States reasserted its leadership position in the global arena and actively pitted itself against the Soviet bloc. This required fostering economic and political alliances with friendly nations as well as threatening to use (or using) armed intervention against others.

Weighing Public Opinion

Of course, during any debate about armed intervention, it is necessary to gauge public opinion among the citizens of the nation that may do the intervening. Governments must consider an important political question: Will the public approve of spending large sums of its own money and putting its military forces at risk to aid another country?

During and immediately after the Kosovo crisis, a number of polls indicated that a majority of Americans did not approve of their nation's involvement. In part because of this high rate of disapproval, ongoing US involvement in Kosovo remained limited.

At the same time, many analysts believe that a decision over whether to intervene in a given situation is too often made strictly on the grounds of self-interest. One such analyst is Rieff. He has pointed out that it is common for public pressure, in the form of election cycles and other domestic distractions, to determine the course of foreign policy. Rieff writes:

> *There have been times ... when it has appeared that Western involvements came about because the leaders of the Western countries no longer found it politically possible to get up at a press conference before a television audience and say in effect, "Sorry about the starving X's or the ethnically cleansed Y's. It's just awful what's happening to them, but frankly they don't have any oil, nor are those that oppress them a threat to us. So you, Mr. and Mrs. Voter, will have to continue to watch the slaughter on the evening news until it burns itself out."*

One possible reason behind this type of cynical decision-making is the potential for economic or political gain for the intervening country. For instance, some Americans developed the belief that the government's purpose in intervening in Kosovo was not truly grounded in humanitarian concerns alone. Instead, they suspected that its main purpose was as a gesture to support the interests of America's European allies and to maintain the legitimacy of the NATO alliance.

Some Americans also saw cynical motives behind US involvement in the botched efforts to stop ethnic massacres in Rwanda. They accused the American government of being as interested in reports of possible oil sources there as it was in strictly humanitarian goals—and furthermore alleged that a major reason for the West's noninvolvement had been relative indifference to the plight of Africans.

Policies of Containment

During both Bush administrations, American policy took a much more aggressive stance toward intervention than it had in previous times, but with very different results. In the first case, George H. W. Bush declared a policy of containment in Iraq that succeeded in curtailing weapons development and Saddam Hussein's murderous repression of dissidents, Kurds, and other people there. In theory, the policy of the first Bush administration should have made further armed aggression unnecessary, though as later events transpired, the containment policy did not seem to have worked as planned.

Walzer writes that, in his opinion, the Iraq War occurred because of a policy that stressed spreading one ideology (democracy through regime change) over containing another (Saddam Hussein's repressive rule). That wasn't the only reason, however. Walzer adds that the Bush administration likely invaded Iraq because containment was becoming less and less effective: "The containment of Saddam's Iraq began as a multilateral enterprise, but in the end it was the Americans who were doing almost all the work … Had containment been an international project, American power might also have been contained within it."

The Role of Global Opinion

Perhaps the final element in the argument against armed intervention—but certainly not the least important factor—is the very real possibility of condemnation, or even overt retaliation, on the part of other nations or groups. When a nation uses armed intervention to achieve strategic objectives beyond humanitarian purposes, it runs the risk of losing both real and apparent legitimacy in the eyes of the global community.

This, in turn, can have a dramatic impact on international relations. Political science scholar Alexander L. George, in his essay "The Role of Force in Democracy," explains: "[O]ne finds in history many cases in which threats of force or

Protesters in Kabul, Afghanistan, on April 26, 2016, hold up signs opposing the role of the United Nations in the country.

the actual use of force were ineffective or seriously aggravated disputes between states."

Experiences in Southeast Asia and elsewhere have strengthened such conclusions. The more recent war on terrorism is another obvious example. The proactive stance taken by the United States to combat terrorism is widely perceived, in the Middle East and elsewhere, as having purposes other than the stated goals of preserving national security and containing dictatorships.

In the aftermath of the September 11 terrorist attacks, there was an enormous international outpouring of goodwill and sympathy toward the United States. However, numerous polls—and evidence in ongoing news reports—demonstrate that much of this goodwill was seriously eroded by the US intervention in Iraq, which was controversial from the start.

One ongoing poll is the Pew Global Attitudes Project, sponsored by the Pew Charitable Trusts. This poll is the largest series in history of long-term, multinational surveys focusing on worldwide issues. Since 2002, the project has conducted more than five hundred thousand interviews in sixty-four countries. Andrew Kohut, president of the Pew Charitable Trusts, reported on the findings in March 2010, at a session of the US House of Representative's Foreign Affairs Subcommittee on International Organizations, Human Rights, and Oversight. He noted that, overall, the survey indicated a marked rise in anti-Americanism around the world for much of the past decade. This effect was particularly strong in many countries following the invasion of Iraq, and world opinion of the United States remained low through 2008.

In 2009, however, the Pew organization noted the beginning of a revival of America's positive image, apparently reflecting confidence in the new president, Barack Obama. By the middle of 2009, opinions about the United States were roughly as positive as they had been at the beginning of the decade, before

George W. Bush took office. Kohut noted that this change was especially noticeable in European nations that had long expressed dissatisfaction with US foreign policy. He stated, "For example, America's favorable rating in Germany jumped from 31% in 2008 to 64% in 2009. A comparable increase in positive opinion was apparent in France (42% to 75%). While improvements in the US's ratings were most dramatic in Western Europe, changes in a positive direction were [also] apparent in major Asian and Latin American countries and elsewhere."

The year 2018 painted a very different picture. "America's global image plummeted following the election of President Donald Trump, amid widespread opposition to his administration's policies and a widely shared lack of confidence in his leadership," Pew analysts reported. A total of 50 percent of people surveyed across twenty-five countries had favorable views of the United States, compared to 43 percent with unfavorable views. Seventy percent of respondents expressed "no confidence" in President Trump, and 70 percent said that the United States works very little or not at all to take into account other countries' interests.

Opinions about when, where, and if military intervention is appropriate shift with every conflict and will continue to shift. The specific way in which a particular conflict is addressed—whether by military or nonmilitary means—plays a critical role in determining the success of any strategy.

Chapter Six

MEASURING THE IMPACT OF INTERVENTION

A military intervention has the potential to alter world events on a massive scale. If successful, an intervention can defend human rights, protect economic and political interests, defend national security, or bring an end to violence. When interventions fail, however, they can lead to long military entanglements, devastating violence, discord among the international community, or economic woes for any or all parties involved. In most cases, though, the results are not so easy to measure. While an intervention might be successful in some respects, it may have fallen short in others.

For example, the multilateral intervention in Kosovo had, on the one hand, some severely negative effects. On the other hand, political scholar Michael

Opposite: On June 13, 1999, British paratroopers walk the streets of Pristina, Yugoslavia. They are part of the NATO intervention in the area as conflict continues.

Bhatia noted in 2000 that the intervention had stopped virtually all the violence in the region, and relatively quickly. He added that it had also benefited the region's economic situation: "NATO's intervention has permitted the reemergence of Kosovo's economic ties with Albania and the rest of Europe. In addition, the influx of international assistance, not to mention international aid workers and civil servants, has jump-started the service sector and led to a construction boom."

The many ways in which armed intervention has an impact on the world are difficult to quantify or predict. Some results, however, are to be expected. Interventions can, generally, lead to increases in violence; increases in refugee populations; severe economic consequences, including property destruction, depression, and unemployment; changes in relationships among nations and organizations; and changes in domestic public opinion.

Increasing Numbers of Refugees

One serious and all-too-frequent impact of armed intervention is a dramatic increase in refugee populations. Conflict, whether internal or caused by intervention from outside, often results in mass movements across national borders by desperate civilians in search of safe havens.

The US Committee for Refugees and Immigrants estimates that sixty million people around the globe have been "forcibly displaced" from their homes—and that only 0.1 percent of them will have the opportunity to start a new life. Among the countries that have seen the most displaced persons are Sudan, Myanmar, the Democratic Republic of the Congo, Somalia, Iraq, Iran, Colombia, and Cuba.

Even if refugees find protection away from danger zones, they typically must take shelter in huge camps that allow only

Devastating Costs

I nevitably, any armed intervention will have a serious aftermath. Though there may be gains for some parties and perhaps for the world in general, there can also be significant costs, including financial losses, devastation of land and property, loss of territory, and the human costs of death, injury, displacement, and the destruction of ways of life.

History is full of examples of such costs. The intervention in Korea resulted in some four million casualties, roughly half of them civilians. Well over four hundred thousand South Korean and UN troops died, with the same number of people missing or abducted. Losses among North Korea and its allies are estimated at two million casualties.

More recently, violence continues to rage around the world. One prominent example is the decades-long conflict involving Israel and some of its neighbors. Another is Russia's intervention in Chechnya and Dagestan, where efforts to achieve independence were met with aggressive intervention by Russian troops. One consequence of the latter incursion has been a violent backlash against Russia, including a string of deadly suicide bombings.

One observer of the situation in Chechnya and Dagestan is Ralph Peters, a retired US Army lieutenant colonel whose comments on the military and current affairs have been widely published. In a piece for the *New York Post*, Peters contended that the hard line taken by Russia's then–prime minister (and now president) Vladimir Putin had been notably unsuccessful. Peters wrote, "Putin's done all he can short of outright genocide. His posture's been as tough and uncompromising as that of his … enemies. Yet, enduring success continues to elude him. The terror campaign persists … There will be no victors. Only more casualties. [The] problem has no solution."

Refugees from the genocide in Sudan look through a fence at a refugee camp in southern Chad on March 15, 1999.

bare survival, hence are not suitable for long-term use. The result is widespread hardship and heartbreak; the refugees, who are overwhelmingly poor, remain in dire need of food, physical protection, and medical care, as well as education and financial aid.

Compounding the problem is the duration of the emergency: sometimes the refugees' situation is far from temporary. What at first seemed like a short-term crisis can drag on for years. If a stable government cannot be formed in the refugees' homeland, or if environmental damage precludes their return, people in the camps may not be able to leave for years, if at all. This is true for the many people from Darfur who have been living in refugee camps for more than a decade. In addition, some countries that provide shelter to refugees have laws that prohibit the same individuals from working or becoming citizens, as is the case for Rohingya refugees in Bangladesh.

The refugees from a given conflict are not the only ones who suffer in such situations, of course. The host countries are also placed in difficult positions. Caring for huge numbers of people in desperate need invariably creates an enormous economic and social burden. As a result, some nations are simply unwilling to shelter refugees at all, while others may be forced to turn refugees away.

In recent years, serious refugee problems have arisen in the wake of armed interventions. Although not necessarily confined to a specific region, many of the most intractable problems have occurred in Africa and the Middle East.

The UN Refugee Agency (UNHCR) reported that the situation following the Gulf Wars created the largest single refugee migration in history. Well over two million people, mainly Iraqi Kurds, were housed in temporary camps. Thousands of them, primarily women and children, have died of malnutrition and exposure, as well as disease and unsanitary conditions, due to lack of clean water. While some Iraq War refugees have been able to return home, more were displaced during the violent insurgency by extremist group ISIS.

Prolonged exile can have a crushing impact on a person's sense of dignity and self-worth. With any financial savings or resources depleted, many refugees resort to negative coping mechanisms in order to survive. Problems like school dropouts, child labor, domestic violence, trafficking, and exploitation can affect refugee communities.

Diplomatic Consequences

Another almost-certain impact of military intervention is approval or disapproval by other nations. These reactions may or may not significantly affect international diplomatic and political relationships. If a nation is powerful enough, the disapproval of a smaller, weaker country may not be of overriding concern. However, considering the interlocking nature of the global economy and political arena, even the strongest countries need to consider the opinions of others.

Between 1989 and 2001, the United States sent significant military forces to foreign lands about once every eighteen months on average, such that intervention became something of a standard weapon of US foreign policy. More recently, that policy has softened considerably, focusing primarily on Afghanistan and Iraq, two regions of particular concern, where the incursions and years-long occupations have strived to create stable and lasting governments, among other goals.

Unsurprisingly, this changing focus polarized opinion within the United States and around the world. Though Obama professed a desire to work toward troop withdrawals, progress on those efforts took time, and Obama's approach drew criticism from the then-president of Iran Mahmoud Ahmadinejad in 2009:

> It is not acceptable that some who are several thousands of kilometers away from the Middle East would send their troops for military intervention and for spreading war, bloodshed, aggression, terror and intimidation in the whole region while blaming the protests of nations in the region, that are concerned about their fate and their national security, as a move against peace and as interference in others' affairs.

Consequences at Home

The potential economic and political consequences of armed intervention in the intervening country must figure in considerations of the lasting impact of such ventures. US involvement in Iraq and Afghanistan was, at its height, a major drain on the US economy, as the occupation of Afghanistan was for the Soviets. Some speculation has been that, if overseas military actions have a deep and long-lasting negative impact on the American economy, China—an economic competitor to the United States on the world stage—will likely gain considerable ground. This might naturally rebound and affect the economic health of the United States still more, perhaps to the point of allowing China to successfully challenge the United States as an economic, political, and military superpower.

At the same time, several other nations, among them Japan, France, Germany, and England, have relatively robust economies and/or significant military capabilities. Still others, such as India and Brazil, are steadily gaining regional strength as well. Another factor in the mix, meanwhile, is the coalition known as the European Union (EU). Although it is still a long way from being a cohesive force in the world, the EU is seen as a great power in its own right, particularly in economic affairs.

For the moment, however, the United States continues to dominate the global arena. Its gross domestic product almost equals the GDPs of the next three nations combined: China, Japan, and Germany. Related to this domination is also the United States' huge budget for military spending, which far exceeds that of other nations.

Looking Ahead

As a result of many factors, some of them subject to change, the power of the United States to intervene militarily in the affairs of other nations remains the greatest in the world. Such possibilities, of course, are very much on the minds of many Americans. This comes back to the question of proportionality: Can overseas interventions—in the name of spreading democracy, for humanitarian concerns, or to support any other reason—be worth the potential consequences in terms of future concerns over economics, security, and other issues?

The Avenue of Nations approaching the United Nations Palace in Geneva, Switzerland, is lined with the flags of UN member countries.

Historically, the answer to this has generally been yes, especially in the case of humanitarian intervention. In fact, there often is broad support across party and ideological lines to favor such aid. A prominent political commentator and foreign policy adviser, Robert Kagan, has taken note of this. He comments that "when there is a perceived intersection between a failed state, a potential humanitarian catastrophe and a possible risk to regional or US security," Americans will generally approve of intervention. He goes on to point out that sometimes there is little choice: "As a theoretical matter it's easy to say we're not going to get involved. But as a practical matter, because everything has implications beyond itself, it's not so easy to avoid."

The factors that go into making momentous decisions about intervention—increases in violence and refugee populations, changes in relationships among nations and domestic public opinion, and more—are not only closely interconnected, they are also highly unpredictable. Furthermore, history and politics are never static; indeed, they are in a constant state of flux and change.

As global power relations shift, new leaders ascend to power, and different conflicts emerge, the world will face new and challenging dilemmas regarding whether military intervention is ethical, necessary, unavoidable, or all of the above. Each conflict presents its own challenges, and the actors involved influence any decisions to a great degree. Whether military intervention will remain a key tool used by the United States and other nations around the world remains to be seen.

Glossary

casualty A person who has died.

coalition A temporary alliance of nations, groups, or persons.

colonialism Control or a policy advocating control by a political or national power over a region or people.

diplomacy Civilized, formal political discussions and agreements among countries.

embargo A block on trade.

embezzlement To take something, such as money, illegally for one's own use.

espionage The act of spying.

ethnic cleansing The persecution, imprisonment, or widespread murder of an ethnic minority group.

expansionism A practice or policy whereby a nation seeks to make its territory larger.

extradite To turn over an alleged criminal to another jurisdiction or nation for prosecution.

genocide The intentional and systematic murder of a group based on racial, ethnic, cultural, or religious prejudice.

import duty A tax charged on goods being brought into a country.

incursion A violent or hostile entrance into a country or territory.

intervention The interference of one nation in the affairs of another.

money laundering The illegal transference of money.

mujahideen An Arabic term for warriors or independence fighters.

multilateral Involving more than two nations or parties.

pacifist A person who opposes all war and violence.

racketeering The act of obtaining money illegally, through intimidation for example.

sovereignty The idea that nations have an absolute right to defend their physical territory against invasion.

subsidize To promote or help someone or something using public money.

trafficking Illegal commercial activity.

unilateral Involving one nation or party.

Further Information

Books

Cannon, Martin. *Conflict and Intervention*. Oxford, UK: Oxford
University Press, 2015.

Partridge, Elizabeth. *Boots on the Ground: America's War in Vietnam*.
New York: Viking, 2018.

Schmermund, Elizabeth. *The Persian Gulf War and the War in Iraq*.
New York: Enslow Publishing, 2016.

Smith, David. *Causes and Effects of 20th Century Wars*. Oxford, UK:
Oxford University Press, 2015.

Websites

Foreign Affairs
https://www.foreignaffairs.com
This publication on international relations shares analyses and opinions
from a wide range of experts from around the globe.

The *New York Times* Upfront
http://teacher.scholastic.com/scholasticnews/indepth/upfront/index.asp
This news magazine for kids and teens offers up the latest news in a
format that's optimized for young readers.

The United Nations

http://www.un.org

The United Nations' website offers up articles, news, reports, and insights on military interventions and UN policies regarding armed conflicts and interventions around the world.

Videos

Barack Obama Defends US Military Intervention in Libya

https://www.theguardian.com/world/2011/mar/29/barack-obama-us-speech-libya

In this video, US president Barack Obama explains why the United States felt obligated to intervene in the 2011 conflict in Libya.

ISIS: The "Unintended Consequences" of the US-Led War on Iraq

https://www.foreignpolicyjournal.com/2015/03/23/isis-the-unintended-consequences-of-the-us-led-war-on-iraq

This video from VICE News features an interview with President Barack Obama about how the invasion of Iraq generated unexpected consequences.

Military Interventions in the Broader Middle East: Effects on Nation Building and Education

https://www.brookings.edu/events/military-interventions-in-the-broader-middle-east-effects-on-nation-building-and-education

General Sir David Richards, former chief of defense staff of the British Armed Forces, talks about how a military intervention can affect a nation in an interview with the Brookings Doha Center.

Organizations

Canadian Centre for International Justice

312 Laurier Avenue East
Ottawa, ON K1N 1H9
Canada
(613) 230-6114
https://www.ccij.ca

This organization works to help survivors of conflict, torture, and genocide find justice on the international stage.

Canadian Global Affairs Institute

Suite 1800, 421-7th Avenue SW
Calgary, AB T2P 4K9
Canada
(613) 288-2529
https://www.cgai.ca

This organization brings together the work of scholars and experts in global affairs to "help Canadians better understand their role on the world stage."

Human Rights Watch

350 Fifth Avenue, 34th Floor
New York, NY 10118
(212) 290-4700
http://www.hrw.org

Human Rights Watch is a leading nongovernmental organization that promotes human rights on an international scale. It works to document and prevent genocide, torture, capital punishment, and child labor, among other causes.

North Atlantic Treaty Organization

Boulevard Léopold III/Leopold III-laan, B-1110

Brussels, Belgium

+32 2 707 5041

https://www.nato.int

NATO is a political and military alliance between twenty-nine countries. Its website offers a history of key events in international relations and details NATO's approach to peacefully resolving disputes.

UNICEF USA

125 Maiden Lane

New York, NY 10038

(800) 367-5437

https://www.unicefusa.org

The United Nations Children's Fund seeks to protect children threatened by poverty, conflict, and hunger around the world.

United Nations Refugee Agency

Case Postale 2500

CH-1211 Genève 2 Dépôt

Switzerland

+41 22 739 8111

http://www.unhcr.org

The UNHCR protects and supports refugee victims of war, genocide, natural disasters, and other catastrophic events throughout the world. UNHCR received Nobel Peace Prizes in 1954 and 1981.

Bibliography

Ahmed, Kaamil. "Local Aid Groups Want More of a Say in the Rohingya Refugee Response." IRIN, September 18, 2018. https://www.irinnews.org/news-feature/2018/09/18/local-aid-groups-want-more-say-rohingya-refugee-response.

Albright, Madeleine K. "The End of Intervention." *New York Times*, August 11, 2008. http://www.nytimes.com/2008/06/11/opinion/11albright.html.

Ali, Rushanara. "One Year On, a Million Rohingya Refugees Still Fear for Their Lives." *Guardian* (UK), August 16, 2018. https://www.theguardian.com/commentisfree/2018/aug/16/rohingya-refugees-bangladesh-camps-international-aid.

Alterman, Eric. "'Blowback,' the Prequel." *Nation*, October 25, 2001. https://www.thenation.com/article/blowback-prequel.

"A More Secure World: Our Shared Responsibility." Report of the United Nations Secretary General High-level Panel on Threats, Challenges and Change, February 2005. http://www.un.org/ar/peacebuilding/pdf/historical/hlp_more_secure_world.pdf.

Amr, Wafa. "UNHCR Sees Deepening Needs Among Iraqi Refugees Even as World Interest Wanes." UNHCR News Stories, March 30, 2010. http://www.unhcr.org/4bb216439.html.

Annan, Kofi. "Balance State Sovereignty with Individual Sovereignty." Speech before the UN General Assembly, September 20, 1999. http://users.lmi.net/wfanca/pp_annan_on_sov.html.

Baker, Peter, and Michael Tackett. "Trump Says His 'Nuclear Button' Is 'Much Bigger' Than North Korea's." *New York Times*, January 2, 2018. https://www.nytimes.com/2018/01/02/us/politics/trump-tweet-north-korea.html.

Barrett, Laurence I., Johanna McGeary, and James Kelly. "Sanctions as a Symbol." *Time*, January 11, 1982. http://www.time.com/time/magazine/article/0,9171,925178,00.html.

Beaubien, Jason. "In Bangladeshi Camps, Rohingya Refugees Try to Move Forward with Their Lives." NPR, August 30, 2018. https://www.npr.org/2018/08/30/643008438/in-bangladeshi-camps-rohingya-refugees-try-to-move-forward-with-their-lives.

Bhatia, Michael. "Intervention Offers No Solution for Kosovo." Global Beat Syndicate, New York University Center for War, Peace, and the News Media, September 19, 2000. http://www.bu.edu/globalbeat/ syndicate/Bhatia091900.html.

Blake, Aaron. "The Trump Doctrine Sounds Suspiciously like the Bush Doctrine." *Washington Post*, April 10, 2017. https://www.washingtonpost.com/news/the-fix/wp/2017/04/10/the-trump-doctrine-sounds-suspiciously-like-the-bush-doctrine/?utm_term=.0f0f72dbc83d.

Brands, H. W., ed. *The Use of Force After the Cold War.* College Station, TX: Texas A&M Press, 2005.

Brown, Brigadier General John S. "Introduction." *The United States Army in Somalia, 1992–1994.* http://www.history.army.mil/brochures/Somalia/Somalia.htm.

Burke, Kathleen. "Britain and Germany: From Ally to Enemy."
    Lecture Transcript, April 2005. http://www.gresham.ac.uk/
    event.asp?EventId=302&PageId=108.

Burns, Nicholas. "President Trump Launches Diplomatic Warfare
    with America's Closest Allies." Harvard Kennedy School, Belfer
    Center for Science and International Affairs, July 13, 2018.
    https://www.belfercenter.org/publication/president-trump-
    launches-diplomatic-warfare-americas-closest-allies.

Carothers, Thomas. "Promoting Democracy and Fighting
    Terror." *Foreign Affairs*, January/February, 2003. http://
    www.carnegieendowment.org/publications/index.
    cfm?fa=view&id=1154.

"Charter of the United Nations." United Nations. Accessed November
    6, 2011. http://www.un.org/en/documents/charter/index.shtml.

Chollet, Derek, and James Goldgeier. *America Between the Wars*.
    Philadelphia: Perseus, 2008.

Clarke, Walter, and Jeffrey Herbst. "Somalia and the Future of
    Humanitarian Intervention." *Foreign Affairs*, March/April 1996.
    https://www.foreignaffairs.com/articles/somalia/1996-03-01/
    somalia-and-future-humanitarian-intervention.

Cohen, Zachary, Michelle Kosinski, and Barbara Starr. "Trump's
    Barrage of Attacks 'Beyond Belief,' Reeling NATO Diplomats
    Say." CNN, July 12, 2018. https://www.cnn.com/2018/07/11/
    politics/trump-nato-diplomats-reaction/index.html.

Connors, Will. "Nigeria Turns over Disputed Land to Cameroon." *New York Times*, August 14, 2008. http://www.nytimes. com/2008/08/15/world/africa/15nigeria.html.

Dearden, Lizzie. "Almost 10,000 Yazidis 'Killed or Kidnapped in Isis Genocide but True Scale of Horror May Never Be Known.'" *Independent* (UK), May 9, 2017. https://www.independent. co.uk/news/world/middle-east/isis-islamic-state-yazidi-sex- slaves-genocide-sinjar-death-toll-number-kidnapped-study-un- lse-a7726991.html.

Eisenhower, Dwight D. "Military Industrial Complex Speech." Yale Law School Avalon Project, January 1961. http://avalon.law.yale. edu/20th_century/eisenhower001.asp.

Ellis, Charles Howard. *The Origin Structure & Working of the League of Nations*. Clark, NJ: Lawbook Exchange, 2003.

"Excerpt of High Level Panel's Report." Global Policy Reform, December 2, 2004. http://www.globalpolicy.org/component/ content/article/154/26051.html

Feaver, Peter. "Obama's Embrace of the Bush Doctrine and the Meaning of 'Imminence.'" Foreign Policy, February 5, 2013. https://foreignpolicy.com/2013/02/05/obamas-embrace-of-the- bush-doctrine-and-the-meaning-of-imminence.

Ferguson, Niall. *Colossus*. New York: Penguin, 2004.

Foer, Franklin. "Economic Sanctions." *Slate*, September 14, 1996. http://www.slate.com/id/1034.

"Full Text of Ahmadinejad's Speech to the UN General Assembly," *Salem (OR) News* (Haaretz Service), September 23, 2009. http://www.salem-news.com/articles/september232009/iran_pres_un_9-23-09.php.

Gakidou, Emmanuela, and Christopher J. L. Murray. "Fifty Years of Violent War Deaths from Vietnam to Bosnia: Analysis of Data from the World Health Survey Programme." Institute for Health Metrics and Evaluation, University of Washington, June 2008. http://www.healthdata.org/research-article/fifty-years-violent-war-deaths-vietnam-bosnia-analysis-data-world-health-survey.

Gaynor, Tim. "More International Support Needed for Rohingya Refugees in Bangladesh, Say UN and World Bank Chiefs." UNHCR, July 2, 2018. http://www.unhcr.org/news/latest/2018/7/5b3a40264/international-support-needed-rohingya-refugees-bangladesh-say-un-world.html.

"GBD Results Tool." Institute for Health Metrics and Evaluation, University of Washington, 2018. http://ghdx.healthdata.org/gbd-results-tool.

George, Alexander L. "The Role of Force in Democracy." *The Use of Force After the Cold War*. Edited by H. W. Brands. College Station, TX: Texas A&M Press, 2005.

Gladstone, Rick. "Trump Administration Defends Cuba Embargo at U.N., Reversing Obama." *New York Times*, November 1, 2017. https://www.nytimes.com/2017/11/01/world/americas/cuba-un-us-embargo.html.

Glossop, Ronald J. *Confronting War: An Examination of Humanity's Most Pressing Problem*. Jefferson, NC: McFarland & Co., 2001.

Gordon, Joy. "Cool War." *Harper's*, November 2002. http://www.harpers.org/archive/2002/11/0079384.

Hamilton, Rebecca J. "The Responsibility to Protect: From Document to Doctrine—But What of Implementation?" *Harvard Human Rights Journal*, Spring 2006. http://www.law.harvard.edu/students/orgs/hrj/iss19/hamilton.shtml.

Hauss, Charles. "Military Intervention." Beyond Intractability, August 2003. http://www.beyondintractability.org/essay/military_intervention.

"Head of Human Rights Fact-Finding Mission on Myanmar Urges Security Council to Ensure Accountability for Serious Violations Against Rohingya." United Nations, October 24, 2018. https://www.un.org/press/en/2018/sc13552.doc.htm.

Hedges, Chris. *War Is a Force That Gives Us Meaning*. New York: Public Affairs, 2002.

———. *What Every Person Should Know About War*. New York: Free Press, 2003.

Hehir, J. Bryan. "The Moral Dimension in the Use of Force." *The Use of Force After the Cold War*. Edited by H. W. Brands. College Station, TX: Texas A&M Press, 2005.

Hitz, Frederick P. *Why Spy?* New York: Thomas Dunne, 2008.

Hook, Steven W., and John Spanier. *American Foreign Policy Since World War II*. Washington, DC: CQ Press, 2000.

Hudson, David. "President Obama Makes a Statement on the Crisis in Iraq." Obama White House Archives, August 7, 2014. https://obamawhitehouse.archives.gov/blog/2014/08/07/president-obama-makes-statement-iraq.

"Iraq War Illegal, Says Annan." BBC News, September 16, 2004. http://news.bbc.co.uk/2/hi/middle_east/3661134.stm.

Jaffe, Greg, Josh Dawsey, and Carol D. Leonnig. "Ahead of NATO and Putin Summits, Trump's Unorthodox Diplomacy Rattles Allies." *Washington Post*, July 6, 2018. https://www.washingtonpost.com/politics/ahead-of-nato-and-putin-summits-trumps-unorthodox-diplomacy-rattles-allies/2018/07/06/16c7aa4e-7006-11e8-bd50-b80389a4e569_story.html?utm_term=.ae344efd4964.

Kinzer, Stephen. *Overthrow*. New York: Henry Holt, 2003.

Kohut, Andrew. "Reviving America's Global Image." Pew Global Trust, March 5, 2010. http://pewglobal.org/commentary/display.php?AnalysisID=1072.

"Korean War Casualties." *Hutchinson Encyclopedia*. Accessed March 9, 2011. http://encyclopedia.farlex.com/Korean+War+casualties.

Landler, Mark. "Trump Abandons Iran Nuclear Deal He Long Scorned." *New York Times*, May 8, 2018. https://www.nytimes.com/2018/05/08/world/middleeast/trump-iran-nuclear-deal.html.

"Manuel Noriega Extradited to Panama to Serve Jail Terms." BBC News, December 12, 2011. https://www.bbc.com/news/world-latin-america-16129630.

May, Tiffany. "Helping the Rohingya." *New York Times*, September 29, 2017. https://www.nytimes.com/2017/09/29/world/asia/rohingya-aid-myanmar-bangladesh.html.

McManus, Doyle. "Almost Half the Top Jobs in Trump's State Department Are Still Empty." *Atlantic*, November 4, 2018. https://www.theatlantic.com/politics/archive/2018/11/state-department-empty-ambassador-to-australi/574831.

"Nation-State." United Nations Educational, Scientific, and Cultural Organization. Accessed November 4, 2018. http://www.unesco.org/new/en/social-and-human-sciences/themes/international-migration/glossary/nation-state.

New York Times Editorial Board. "The Trump Administration Is Making War on Diplomacy." *New York Times*, November 18, 2017. https://www.nytimes.com/2017/11/18/opinion/sunday/the-trump-administration-is-making-war-on-diplomacy.html.

Obama, Barack. "Nobel Acceptance Speech." December 14, 2009. http://www.monitor.upeace.org/innerpg.cfm?id_article=680.

Orend, Brian. "War." *Stanford Encyclopedia of Philosophy*. Accessed March 9, 2011. http://plato.stanford.edu/entries/war.

Peters, Ralph. "Why Putin Can't Crush His Islamists." *New York Post*, April 2, 2010. http://www.nypost.com/p/news/opinion/opedcolumnists/why_putin_can_crush_his_islamists_6bhHsU6RAkkC2LUAzwlLdL.

Pfaff, William. "America's National Strategy of Global Intervention." *International Herald-Tribune*, October 15, 2008. http://www.williampfaff.com/modules/news/article.php?storyid=347.

———. "Who Will Emerge as the New Global King of the Hill?" *Sunday Gazette-Mail* (Charleston, West Virginia), February 7,

2010. http://www.allbusiness.com/company-activities-management/
company-structures-ownership/13880069-1.html.

Preble, Christopher. "Striking First: Preemption and Prevention
in International Conflict." The Free Library. Accessed
September 20, 2009. http://www.thefreelibrary.com/
Striking+First%3A+Preemption+and+Prevention+in+International
+Conflict.a0213231919.

"Public Uncertain, Divided over America's Place in the World." Pew
Research Center, May 5, 2016. http://www.people-press.
org/2016/05/05/public-uncertain-divided-over-americas-place-in-
the-world.

"Report of the Special Political and Decolonization Committee." UN
General Assembly Session 62 meeting 121, September 11, 2008.
http://www.undemocracy.com/generalassembly_62/meeting_121.

"Restoring What's Been Lost." US Committee for Refugees and
Immigrants. Accessed November 6, 2018. http://refugees.org/
explore-the-issues/refugees-facts.

Revesz, Rachael. "Donald Trump Has Fired All Foreign US Ambassadors
with Nobody to Replace Them." *Independent* (UK), January 20, 2017.
https://www.independent.co.uk/news/world/americas/donald-trump-
fires-us-ambassadors-no-replacements-a7538256.html.

Rice, Colonel Daniel, and Major John Dehn. "Armed Humanitarian
Intervention and International Law: A Primer for Military
Professionals." *Military Review*, November–December 2007. http://
findarticles.com/p/articles/mi_m0PBZ/is_6_87/ai_n24225701/pg_7.

Richter Paul. "World Breathes Sigh of Relief, Hillary Clinton Says." *Los Angeles Times*, January 28, 2009. http://articles.latimes.com/2009/jan/28/world/fg-clinton28.

Rieff, David. *At the Point of a Gun*. New York: Simon & Schuster, 2005.

————. "At the Point of a Gun: Democratic Dreams and Armed Intervention." Speech before the Carnegie Council, May 4, 2005. http://www.cceia.org/resources/transcripts/5164.html.

Robinson, Peter. "'Tear Down This Wall': How Top Advisers Opposed Reagan's Challenge to Gorbachev—But Lost." US National Archives, Summer 2007. http://www.archives.gov/publications/prologue/2007/summer/berlin.html.

"Ron Paul on Foreign Policy." On the Issues, 2008. http://www.ontheissues.org/2008/Ron_Paul_ Foreign_Policy.htm.

Shear, Michael D. "Trump Will Withdraw U.S. from Paris Climate Agreement." *New York Times*, June 1, 2017. https://www.nytimes.com/2017/06/01/climate/trump-paris-climate-agreement.html.

Shear, Michael D., and Michael R. Gordon. "63 Hours: From Chemical Attack to Trump's Strike in Syria." *New York Times*, April 7, 2017. https://www.nytimes.com/2017/04/07/us/politics/syria-strike-trump-timeline.html.

Soderberg, Nancy. *The Superpower Myth*. Hoboken, NJ: Wiley, 2005.

"Summary of National Security Strategy 2002." The White House, President George W. Bush. Accessed November 6, 2018. https://georgewbush-whitehouse.archives.gov/nsc/nss/2006/sectionV.html.

"Syria Air Strikes: Theresa May Says Action 'Moral and Legal.'" BBC News, April 17, 2018. https://www.bbc.com/news/uk-politics-43775728?intlink_from_url=https://www.bbc.com/news/topics/cme1yzdkllxt/syria-air-strikes&link_location=live-reporting-story.

Tepperman, Jonathan. "Fighting Wars of Peace." *Newsweek International*, December 22, 2008. http://www.newsweek.com/id/174523.

US Congress, Committee on International Relations, Special Subcommittee on Investigations. "Oil Fields as Military Objectives: A Feasibility Study." Prepared by the Congressional Research Service, 94th Congress, 1st session, August 21, 1975 (Washington, DC: US Government Printing Office, 1975), Parts I and II, 1–39. http://www.mtholyoke.edu/acad/intrel/Petroleum/fields.htm.

Walzer, Michael. "Arguing About War." Speech before the Carnegie Council, February 28, 2006. http://www.cceia.org/resources/transcripts/5326.html.

———. *Just and Unjust Wars: A Moral Argument with Historical Illustrations*. New York: Basic Books, 2006.

———. "Regime Change and Just War." *Dissent*, Summer 2006. http://www.dissentmagazine.org/article/?article=663.

Watkins, Eli, and Maegan Vazquez. "Trump Threatens Nuclear Buildup Until Other Nations 'Come to Their Senses.'" CNN, October 24, 2018. https://www.cnn.com/2018/10/22/politics/donald-trump-russia-china-inf/index.html.

Weekly Standard editors. "Return of the Bush Doctrine?" *Weekly Standard*, October 1, 2018. https://www.weeklystandard.com/the-editors/return-of-the-bush-doctrine.

Westcott, Ben. "Donald Trump's Unconventional Diplomacy Is Pushing China and Japan Closer Together." CNN, October 25, 2018. https://www.cnn.com/2018/10/24/asia/japan-china-us-trump-intl/index.html.

Wike, Richard, Bruce Stokes, Jacob Poushter, Laura Silver, Janell Fetterolf, and Kat Devlin. "Trump's International Ratings Remain Low, Especially Among Key Allies." Pew Research Center, Global Attitudes & Trends, October 1, 2018. http://www.pewglobal.org/2018/10/01/trumps-international-ratings-remain-low-especially-among-key-allies/#interactive.

Williams, Ian. "Ban Ki Moon and R2P." Foreign Policy in Focus, August 3, 2009. http://www.fpif.org/articles/ban_ki_moon_and_r2p.

"The World: The Intervention Issue." *Time*, January 20, 1975. http://www.time.com/time/magazine/article/0,9171,912693-3,00.html#ixzz0fvfw201h.

Zenko, Micah. "Obama's Final Drone Strike Data." Council on Foreign Relations, January 20, 2017. https://www.cfr.org/blog/obamas-final-drone-strike-data.

Index

Kissinger, Henry, 38
Korean War, 19–22, **20**, 115
Kosovo crisis, 48–49, **90**, 91–92,
    99, 107–108, 113–114

League of Nations, 16–18, 106
legal avenues to peace, 8, 57–59,
    52
Liberia, 17, 62
Libya, 62–64, 67, 81

military-industrial complex, 23
Milosevic, Slobodan, 49, 91–92
Myanmar, 68, 70, 114

national security, 40–42, 76–84
national territory, defending, 89–92
Nicaragua, 58–59
Nigeria, 59
Nixon, Richard, 25, 36
nongovernmental organizations
    (NGOs), 70–71, 97
nonintervention, policy of, 102–106
Noriega, Manuel, 43–46
North Atlantic Treaty Organization
    (NATO), 48–49, 55, 91–92,
    99, 108, **112**
North Korea, 21, 55, 115

Obama, Barack, 6, 9, 49, 81–82,
    85–86, 110, 118
    diplomacy under, 53–54, 56,
        63, 85

oil embargo of 1970s, 35–38, **37**
OPEC, 35–36
Operation Desert Storm, 37–40
Operation Just Cause, 43–46,
    44–45

pacifism, 73, 96
Pakistan, 27, 53, 81–82
Panama, 43–46, **44–45**
Paul, Ron, 103
political reasons, intervention for,
    42–47
Powell, Colin, 99
preemption vs. prevention, 76
proportionality, 97–99
protests, 24–25, **61**, **94**, **109**
Prussia, 12–13
public opinion, 103, 107–108
Putin, Vladimir, 55, 115

Qaddafi, Muammar, 64, 67

Reagan, Ronald, 30, 58, 67
refugees, **50**, **69**, **90**, **102**, 114–117,
    116, 121
regime change, 42–47
Rieff, David, 104–105, **105**, 107
Rohingya, 68, **69**, 116
Russia, 12, 16, 18, 48, 53, 55–56,
    84, 99, 115
Rwanda genocide, 91–92, 102,
    102, 108

About the Author

Erin L. McCoy is a literature, language, and cultural studies educator and an award-winning photojournalist and poet. She holds a master of arts degree in Hispanic studies and a master of fine arts degree in creative writing from the University of Washington. She has edited more than two dozen nonfiction books for young adults, including *The Mexican-American War*, *The Israel-Palestine Border Conflict*, and *Poverty: Public Crisis or Private Struggle?* from Cavendish Square Publishing. She is from Louisville, Kentucky.

Adam Woog has written many books for adults, young adults, and children. He has a special interest in history and biography. Woog lives in Seattle, Washington.